ENVIRONMENTAL SAFEGUARD MONITORING FIELD KIT
PROJECT IMPLEMENTATION DIRECTORATE, NEPAL

FEBRUARY 2023

ASIAN DEVELOPMENT BANK

ADB

© 2023 Asian Development Bank
6 ADB Avenue, Mandaluyong City, 1550 Metro Manila, Philippines
Tel +63 2 8632 4444; Fax +63 2 8636 2444
www.adb.org

Some rights reserved. Published in 2023.

ISBN 978-92-9270-047-8 (print); 978-92-9270-048-5 (electronic); 978-92-9270-049-2 (ebook)
Publication Stock No. TIM230051-2
DOI: http://dx.doi.org/10.22617/TIM230051-2

The views expressed in this publication are those of the authors and do not necessarily reflect the views and policies of the Asian Development Bank (ADB) or its Board of Governors or the governments they represent.

ADB does not guarantee the accuracy of the data included in this publication and accepts no responsibility for any consequence of their use. The mention of specific companies or products of manufacturers does not imply that they are endorsed or recommended by ADB in preference to others of a similar nature that are not mentioned.

By making any designation of or reference to a particular territory or geographic area, or by using the term "country" in this document, ADB does not intend to make any judgments as to the legal or other status of any territory or area.

Please contact pubsmarketing@adb.org if you have questions or comments with respect to content, or if you wish to obtain copyright permission for your intended use that does not fall within these terms, or for permission to use the ADB logo.

Corrigenda to ADB publications may be found at http://www.adb.org/publications/corrigenda.

Notes:
In this publication, "$" refers to United States dollars.

Cover design by Bhuvan Adhikari.

On the cover: From the left to right (1) sewer pipe laying, (2) traditional waterspout, and (3) project work (Photos by DB Singh, ADB and PID/KUKL, Nepal).

CONTENTS

TABLES, FIGURES AND BOXES

FOREWORD

The Kathmandu Valley is home to ancient cities with rich cultural heritage, temples and monuments including seven UNESCO World Heritage Sites. They all contribute to the Valley's distinct historic character shaping the cultural identity of its inhabitants and providing immense benefits to the economy.

Over time, the ancient structures have suffered much damage from long exposure to extreme weather conditions, earthquakes, and years of neglect. Such sites are mostly surrounded by dense and dynamic human settlement where urban development pressure is high. Hence, the challenge is to ensure the monuments and old structures are protected during development work as the cities continue to grow. One development work that is especially relevant in this regard is the underground water supply and sewerage pipe laying in the narrow lanes of the old settlements in the Kathmandu Valley without causing damage to the vulnerable structures and disrupting the daily lives of its residents.

The Asian Development Bank (ADB) has published this Environmental Safeguard Monitoring Field Kit to support the Project Implementation Directorate (PID) of the Kathmandu Upatyaka Khanepani Limited (KUKL) in carrying out their work by complying with the environmental safeguard requirements. This practical guide will support PID staff in following a systematic procedure for environmental planning, compliance monitoring, and reporting while implementing the work. The field kit could also be a useful reference document to other stakeholders related to the water supply and sanitation sector.

Let me congratulate Deepak Bahadur Singh, environment specialist, ADB and Nawa Raj Khatiwada, ADB consultant for their dedicated work in publishing this useful guide. I would also like to thank Saswati Belliappa, senior safeguards specialist and Saugata Dasgupta, senior project management specialist, ADB for their support in the preparation of this kit. My gratitude to PID/KUKL and its Safeguard Unit for their valuable feedback in finalizing the document.

I hope this field kit will receive full government attention and will be put into wider use in the sector that may help to protect and preserve the unique environment, vulnerable structures, and cultural heritage while carrying out development works in Nepal.

Arnaud Cauchois
Country Director
Nepal Resident Mission
Asian Development Bank

ACKNOWLEDGMENTS

The Environmental Safeguard Monitoring Field Kit was prepared by the Asian Development Bank (ADB). The purpose of this field kit is to help the Project Implementation Directorate (PID) of the Kathmandu Uptyaka Khanepani Limited, Nepal (KUKL) in following standard environmental safeguard procedure and practices, including environmental management planning, monitoring, and reporting while carrying out water supply and sanitation related infrastructure development works. The Field Kit suggests procedural guide, formats, templates, checklists, samples, and standards for ready reference and use. It is also relevant and helpful as a reference guide to other stakeholders and agencies working in water supply and sanitation infrastructure development. Deepak Bahadur Singh, environment specialist, South Asia Department, ADB authored this publication, with the support of Nawa Raj Khatiwada, environment consultant, ADB. The field kit was prepared under the overall support and guidance provided by Saswati Belliappa, senior safeguards specialist and Saugata Dasgupta, senior project management specialist, South Asia Department, ADB. We acknowledge the valuable inputs provided by Laxmi Pant, chief of the Safeguard Unit, PID and her team in preparation of this field kit. We also acknowledge all who directly and indirectly supported in its publication.

ABBREVIATIONS

ADB	Asian Development Bank
AEC	Archaeologist Expert Committee
BOQ	bill of quantity
CASSC	community awareness and safeguards support consultant
CBO	community-based organization
DDR	due diligence report
DOA	Department of Archaeology
DOR	Department of Roads
DSC	design and supervision consultant
EARF	environmental assessment and review framework
EIA	environmental impact assessment
EMP	environmental management plan
GCC	general condition of contract
GESI	gender equality and social inclusion
GPS	global positioning system
GRM	grievance redress mechanism
HIA	heritage impact assessment
IEE	initial environmental examination
KUKL	Kathmandu Upatyaka Khanepani Limited
MOWS	Ministry of Water Supply
MWSP	Melamchi Water Supply Project
NEA	Nepal Electricity Authority
NGO	nongovernment organization
NTC	notice to correct
O&M	operation and maintenance
OHS	occupational health and safety
PAM	project administration manual
PCC	particular condition of contract
PID	Project Implementation Directorate
PMU	project management unit
PPE	personal protective equipment
REA	rapid environmental assessment
ROW	right-of-way
SEMP	site-specific environmental management plan
SOP	standard operating procedure
SU	safeguard unit
TOR	terms of reference
WWTP	Wastewater treatment plant

Chapter 1
FIELD KIT

A. Purpose

1. The purpose of the Environmental Safeguard Monitoring Field Kit (also referred to hereinafter as "the Kit") is to provide a handy and readily implementable on-the-job field guide to the environment experts, staff of the employer, consultants, and contractors of the Project Implementation Directorate (PID) of Kathmandu Upatyaka Khanepani Limited (KUKL), the public company that manages water supply and sanitation services to the Kathmandu Valley. The Kit aims to assist the PID and related stakeholders in following environmental safeguard requirements at the planning, implementation, and commissioning stages of the water supply and wastewater management systems. To assist the safeguard staff, the Kit provides ready-made formats, templates, outlines, and checklists that the user can readily retrieve from the Annexes. They can also be retrieved by clicking on the hyperlinked word in the soft copy of the main text.

B. Applicability

2. The primary intent of the Kit is to support in environmental safeguard-related activities during the planning, implementation, and operation stages of a project, with focus on monitoring and reporting during work implementation and commissioning. The Kit can be referred to while preparing environmental assessments, heritage impact assessments (HIAs), engineering designs and estimates, bidding and contract documents, and site-specific environmental management plans (SEMPs) (Chapter 3). Also, the Kit is applicable to other stakeholders in general implementing water supply and wastewater management projects.

C. Limitation

3. The scope of this Field Kit is limited to the environmental safeguard measures related to the implementation and operation of water supply (service reservoir tank, bulk distribution system, distribution network) and wastewater treatment and sewer laying works. Measures for the planning stage, particularly on conducting environmental impact assessment (EIA) or initial environmental examination (IEE) is not presented in detail. The Kit does not consider environmental safeguard measures related to headwork and/or intake for water diversion and tunnel works since these structures are beyond the scope of the PID. Meanwhile, the checklists presented in the Kit need to be updated and made project-specific or used in combination with other site-specific checklists.

D. Guide for Field Kit Users

4. The Field Kit has been prepared primarily for the PID to support and guide the user in conducting environmental monitoring and reporting. Its objective is for users to have a common understanding of the monitoring requirements and to maintain the quality of monitoring reports. The main text presents planning, monitoring, and reporting in separate chapters, looking at water supply and wastewater systems separately. The Kit suggests various procedures, formats, and templates for ready use. A user can access these templates simply by hovering the mouse cursor above the hyperlinked word in the soft copy of the main text and clicking to retrieve the required format.

Chapter 2
ENVIRONMENTAL SAFEGUARD DOCUMENT

5. This chapter presents an overview of the key project documents that incorporate the safeguard policies and provisions needed to mobilize the budgetary and human resources to meet the overall objective of environmental management.

A. Engineering Design and Drawing

6. The engineering design provides technical details of the project and serves as a key reference document regarding integrating and implementing specific environmental safeguard measures as suggested by the environmental management plan (EMP). An EMP is an integral part of the approved environmental assessment documents.[1] The environmental assessment is carried out during the feasibility study stage and updated during the detailed engineering design. The proposed EMP recommendations should be incorporated into the detailed project report, with costing for their implementation. The contractor refers to the EMP while preparing the site-specific environmental management plan (SEMP) immediately upon award of contract and before field mobilization. The SEMP is approved by the employer on recommendation of the engineer (the design and supervision consultant in the PID's case). The SEMP must include a base map of the project area, a drawing of structures, environmentally sensitive receptors, site-specific mitigation measure, and monitoring details (location, method, frequency, specifications, responsible agency, budget).

B. Environmental Assessment

7. This Kit covers primarily the monitoring activities to be followed after completion of detailed design and when preparation of the bidding document and contract is initiated. However, it also presents a brief review of the scope of environmental assessment and a typical example of the EMP.[1]

8. An EIA or IEE reviews the existing physical, biological, and socioeconomic environment of the area of influence of the project and predicts the type and scale of possible environmental impacts and occupational health and safety (OHS) issues owing to implementation and operation of the project. Based on this, the prediction of the impacts, as well as the required mitigation measures to avoid, minimize, or compensate such impacts are designed and its implementation plan is prepared as an EMP. A typical EMP matrix includes activity, impact, mitigation measure, monitoring method, parameter to monitor, location of monitoring, frequency of monitoring, responsible agency and cost. The EIA or IEE also suggests communication, consultation, and grievance redress mechanism. The EIA or IEE is approved by the concerned government agency. The EIA is approved by the Ministry of Forests and Environment. The Ministry of Water Supply approves the PID related IEEs. The actions

---

1   Environmental assessment documents include EIAs, IEEs, and short IEEs (as per Nepal's Environmental Protection Rules 2020), and environment due diligence reports (as per Asian Development Bank).

and costs suggested in the EMP are transferred along with the recommended mitigation measures in the detailed project report (DPR). The approved EMP is attached to the bidding and contract documents with the estimated cost in the bill of quantity (BOQ). The contractor prepares a SEMP based on the project EMP vis-à-vis the locational environmental attributes and implements after approval by the employer (PID) on recommendation of the environment consultant of the design and supervision consultant and the community awareness and safeguards support consultant (CASSC).

9. The EIA or IEE preparation for the Asian Development Bank (ADB) is guided by its Safeguard Policy Statement (2009) and, for the borrower, by the Environmental Protection Act (2019) and the Environmental Protection Rule (2020). The content is principally the same for ADB and for the government, but there is some difference in the presentation structure. An outline of the EIA as per ADB requirements is attached in Annex I (A) and outline of the IEE is in Annex I (B). A typical EMP table is attached as Annex I (C). The IEE and EIA structure in the Environmental Protection Rule is presented in its Schedule 11 and 12. The three most important deliverables in the EIA or IEE are (i) the EMP and environmental monitoring plan; (ii) the stakeholder communication, consultation, and disclosure plan, and (iii) grievance redress mechanism. Table 2.1 presents the typical issues considered by the mitigation measures suggested in the EMP in an EIA or IEE.

Table 2.1: Typical Issues Generally Considered in an Environmental Management Plan

Physical Environment	Biological Environment	Sociocultural Environment
- Topsoil management - Spoil management - Excavated soil management - Natural drainage - Air/dust pollution - Water pollution - Noise pollution - Solid waste and construction waste management - Landslide - Flood - Water seepage - River crossing - Sedimentation - Water logging - Access - Impact on archaeological sites and historical buildings - Sludge management - Climate change - Carbon footing - Quarry management - Crusher and batching plants management	- Tree cutting - Compensatory plantation - Ecologically sensitive area - National park and buffer zone - Use of firewood - Habitat loss - Impact on aquatic life - Terrestrial flora and fauna - Avian fauna (birds) - Aquatic fauna	- Loss of land and property - Damage to community infrastructure - Disruption to supply and business loss - Workers' camp and facilities - Health and safety risks and use of personal protective equipment - Injuries and accidents - Emergency management - Traffic management - Community stress, crime, HIV/AIDS - Grievances - Local employment, wages and child labor - Emergency response and disaster preparedness (both workers and community) - Cultural practices - Festival grounds

C. Bidding Document

10. A bidding document is the first source of information for contractors on the environmental compliance requirements while implementing the work in a project. It provides a detailed description of the project, a work specification, and an estimated quantity of work for which procurement is desired. The document should include the EMP requirements with costs. The bidding document that the PID generally uses is the small works standard bidding document of ADB, with a single-stage two-envelop selection method. An outline of a sample bidding document is presented in Annex I (D).

Bill of Quantity

11. The BOQ in a bidding document is where the contractor offers their cost for undertaking a given type of work in a given quantity. It is important that the BOQ also includes the type and quantity of EMP- and OHS-recommended work, with the contractor agreeing to implement those at a proposed rate. The EMP cost can be included in a bidding document using the following three methods:
    (i) **Unit rate with quantity of work** for items that can be quantified and for which the unit rate is available;
    (ii) **Lumpsum** for items that is difficult to quantify, such as water sprinkling to required frequency; and
    (iii) **Provisional sum** for items whose type and cost can be defined only during work implementation (Box 2.1).

Box 2.1: Example of Provisional Sum

Provisional sum includes provision for mitigation measures to deal with unanticipated environmental impacts and social safeguards, such as reinstating or relocating public utilities (telephone/electric poles, transformers, street lighting, unanticipated water supply pipelines, water supply fittings and accessories), supply of potable water to the affected area, reinstatement of unspecified pavements, reinstatement of accidentally damaged structures, and other items not covered by unit rate.

Environmental Management Plan Provisions in the Bill of Quantity

12. Contractors generally do not focus much on allocating sufficient sums to meet EMP and OHS requirements in their bids. It is generally the case in Nepal that either the bidding document does not cover EMP requirements in detail or the bidders quote a minimal amount for EMP and OHS implementation so they can submit the lowest bid to win the contract. The consequence is that the quality of compliance with EMP and OHS requirements has to be seriously compromised during implementation. Hence, the employer needs to ascertain during the bid evaluation that the bidding documents respond to environmental safeguard requirements and that the contractor has allocated sufficient costs to implement them. An outline of sample EMP provisions in a BOQ is presented in Annex I (P) and Annex I (R).

D. Contract Document

13. A contract document is the written agreement between two or more parties defining their roles and describing tasks, conditions, specifications, services, quality, and procedure. The conditions of the contract, which provide the rights, obligations, and responsibilities of the parties concerned in the contract execution, are important. The type of contract that the PID normally uses is attached as part III of the standard bidding document for small work of ADB (Annex I (D)).

14. The conditions to be included in the contract agreement for PID work are discussed in detail in Chapter 3. Box 2.2 presents general items to be covered by a contract document.

Box 2.2: Environmental Safeguard Requirements to be provisioned in a Contract Document

1. Preparation and strict adherence to approved site-specific environmental management plan (SEMP)
2. Qualified environmental and health and safety personnel required to be on-site
3. Plans that the contractor should develop for client approval (SEMP, occupational health and safety, emergency protocol, special measures while working in World Heritage Sites and archaeological areas in the Kathmandu Valley, and workers code of conduct)
4. Prior government approvals and permits
5. Labor camp standards with required facilities
6. Health and safety measures including medical facilities served by full-time medical staff
7. Post-accident management procedure (emergency protocol) and compensation
8. Training on environmental safeguards and safety, and the line of command to workers
9. Monitoring of environmental parameters (noise, air, water, waste), method, and frequency
10. Grievance redress mechanism for activities related to contractors' work
11. Safeguard review mechanism and scoring system on environmental safeguard and safety performance
12. Conditions of site restoration after completion of work and before leaving site by contractor
13. Financial penalties (percentage deduction from the interim bill) for noncompliance, and client's right to implement corrective measures and deduct the cost from the interim bill adding a service charge
14. Reporting requirements
15. Contractor takes sole responsibility for the safeguard performance by its construction team and suppliers.

E. Site-Specific Environmental Management Plan

15. A SEMP, sometimes called a contractor's environmental management plan, is a plan prepared by a contractor before field mobilization.[2] The SEMP is approved by the employer on recommendation of the design and supervision consultant (DSC). The plan is prepared by the contractor following the general EMP in the EIA or IEE and attached to the bidding and contract documents. Essentially, the SEMP is an EMP prepared for each typical section of the work area, covering location-specific environmental characteristics and issues. An outline of a typical SEMP is presented in Annex I (E).

---

2 By making the SEMP and OHS document an integral parts of the contract, the client will have better tools to manage the safeguard performance of their contractors. They will be able to control the contractor's activity and enforce safeguard compliance. (E&S Management, IFC 2014)

F. Occupational Health and Safety Plan

16. The contractor should also submit an OHS plan along with the SEMP. An OHS plan considers facilities and praticies to ensure a healthy and safe living and working environment for workers. Like the EMP, the OHS plan includes activities, potential health and safety issues, safety management requirements, safety monitoring, and reporting along with costs. The cost could be a BOQ cost item or a provisional sum. By making the SEMP and OHS document integral parts of the contract, the client will have better tools to manage the safeguard performance of their contractors. They will be able to control the contractor's activity and enforce safeguard and safety compliance.

G. Heritage Impact Assessment

17. Kathmandu Valley is an ancient settlement with seven World Heritage Sites within a small area of 665 square kilometers. The heritage sites and settlements are closely integrated. The government is responsible for providing the required health and sanitation services to the population irrespective of whether or not they are within the heritage sites. Hence, there may be important artifacts and ancient structures underground in the project area that could be encountered—and could incur damage—during the work. To avoid such unintentional incidents, a heritage impact assessment (HIA) should be prepared by studying and investigating the area using state-of-the-art underground scanning technology and open trenching, and by consulting with archaeologists and the local community. The general structure of the HIA is discussed further in the following chapters (see Annex I (T)) and an HIA framework is presented as Annex II-Form #219.

Chapter 3

ENVIRONMENTAL MONITORING

18. This chapter presents a brief description of effective and cost-effective environmental monitoring practices.

19. The main purpose of environmental monitoring is to verify the effectiveness of environmental protection measures in achieving the results specified in the EMP. When the monitoring indicates that environmental measures are not achieving the expected results, it provides the basis for corrective actions. Monitoring is cost-intensive if not carried out efficiently and effectively, or if it fails to focus on the main risks to the environment. A good monitoring plan chooses the right and cost-effective parameters to monitor using a correct methodology and appropriate equipment (based on the level of precision required), at the right frequency, in the right location.

Figure 3.1: Layout Map with Existing Structure and Sensitive Receptors

Source: DB Singh, Asian Development Bank.

A. Tools and Equipment for Environmental Monitoring

20. All required equipment, tools, and resources should be arranged before monitoring.

Safety of Staff
- Personal protective equipment (PPE) (hardhats, safety boots, reflective jackets)
- Masks and/or face shields
- Gloves
- Hand sanitizer

Reference Map, Document, and Monitoring Checklist
- Topographic land use map or sketch of the site at 1:10,000 or 1:15,000 scale showing all structures, camps, stockpile areas, drainage, and sensitive receptors (rivers, lakes, schools, hospitals, prominent structures, historical monuments, etc.)
- Approved copy of the SEMP and OHS plan
- Measuring tapes (3 meters and 50 meters)
- Plan and cross-section of key structures

Field Measurement
- Form that lists the parameters to be tested
- Sample bottles, specimen pouches, etc. along with the manual for specimen collection
- In terms of dust monitoring equipment, choose testing with portable field equipment or lab testing based on level of significance of impact and resource availability. Measurements shall be taken at the source of dust and pollution, and at the sensitive receptors:

  (i) Deposition gauge (the simplest equipment). This is a cost-effective and reliable method for dust monitoring, consisting of a glass funnel supported by a glass bottle. It does not require power to operate and can be easily carried and positioned

  (ii) Sticky pads. These are adhesive slides mounted on a collection cylinder on a post approximately 2 meters above the ground, normally exposed for 1–2 weeks. Dust influx is captured for subsequent analysis using a sticky pad reader.)

  (iii) A real-time (continuous) dust monitor, which captures dust for up to 8 hours. This can be wall-or fence-mounted or can be fixed on a tripod

- Choose noise monitoring equipment based on importance and resource availability. Measure the noise level at the sensitive receptors by generally using a handheld decibel meter. For critical areas, a continuous noise monitor equipment could be fixed at site.

- Vibration monitoring is a specialized activity and, therefore, needs careful thought if included in the monitoring plan. Vulnerable receptors may be old and heritage buildings prone to structural damage, or a school, temple,

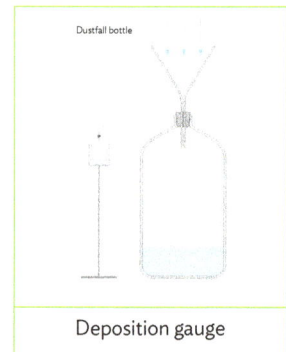

Deposition gauge

Sticky pads

Real-time (continuous) dust monitor

slide prone slopes, where vibration could cause serious impact on structure or people. Vibration monitors can be attached to the structures, and their readings occur at scheduled intervals via a link to a computer.

Decibel meter

- Water quality monitoring should be based on sampling and regular inspections (choose testing with a portable field test kit or lab testing of sample based on the level of significance of impact and resource availability). Typical parameters are pH, turbidity, dissolved oxygen, total suspended solid, total dissolved solid, conductivity, coliform, total organic carbon, and heavy metals (as required). A hatch test kit will help in field water testing. Sampling and lab testing will give an accurate result. A third-party laboratory should be engaged by the contractor(s) to avoid conflict of interest in reporting.

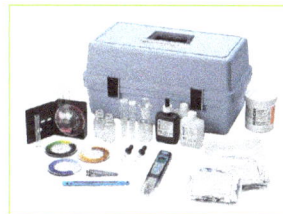

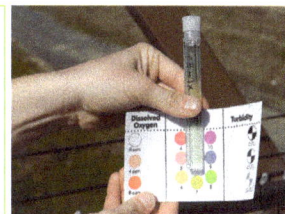

Water pollution field test kit

- Other items those could be used for field measurement include (i) digital camera with an adjustable date, (ii) compass and altitude meter, (iii) measuring tape, (iv) global positioning system (GPS) device, (v) binoculars, and (vi) audio recording device (to use during interviews and consultation). With government permission, it is useful to carry a drone for an overall bird's-eye view of the entire terrain. In addition, subject-matter specialists (biologists) may carry other tools and resources to count, record, and prepare samples for lab verification. The use of tools will also depend on the type and purpose of the monitoring.

B. Preparations for Environmental Monitoring

21. The examiner should be an objective observer, inspector, and interviewer. The examiner should refer to this section before commencing the monitoring process.

Monitoring Checklist with Scoring of Quality of Compliance

22. The score to assign when filling out the monitoring checklist can range from 0 to 5, where 0 = critical, 1 = very poor, 2 = poor, 3 = good, 4 = very good, and 5 = excellent. Alternatively, the monitoring score can follow the performance level as presented in Table 3.1.

Table 3.1: Total Score, Performance Quality, and Possible Measures

Score	Performance Quality	Action to be Taken
Over 90	Excellent	Recommend for reward; this could, for example, be in the form of a public recognition or a certificate of appreciation.
85–90	Very good	Minor improvement in environmental compliance needed.
75–84	Good	Major improvement in environmental compliance needed.
60–74	Poor	Urgent attention needed; convene a meeting with the project manager and send notice to correct, with a copy to the lead contractor's management at their headquarters.
<60	Critical	The design, supervision, and contract management consultant should immediately inform the Project Implementation Directorate about the seriousness of noncompliance. Organize a meeting with the contractor's management. If needed, stop work depending on the level of noncompliance and its seriousness for the environment and safety until corrective measure are taken to the satisfaction of the Engineer.

Some Issues to Consider During Monitoring

(i) Signage in the sites should be intelligible and concise and in both English and the local language. Cautionary and warning signs should be clearly visible with proper graphics. The examiner should check if the signboards are damaged, faded, covered with vegetation, and susceptible to the weather. The examiner should also check whether the signage is located at the appropriate location.

(ii) Safety signage boards should include information regarding fire and electricity hazards; slip, trip, and fall risk; no smoking zones; no entrance areas; etc.

(iii) A first aid box should be available in each work site and camp.

(iv) Uses of PPE in different work environments should be considered (Table 3.2).

(v) Fire extinguishers should be available at the site and should not be expired.

(vi) Safety barricades installed around work area:

a) Hard barricade around work area. As a rule of thumb, this is a minimum 1.22-meter high painted metal post with nylon ropes in three rows or green net having visible cautionary signage.

b) Warning barricades may include woven tape, reflective plastic tape, or any other materials with correct color coding.

c) All barricades should be placed and maintained in a neat and orderly manner and provided with gates for easy access. Corners shall be squared.

Informative and safety signboards. It is important for signages to be clear, concise, and strategically placed to make them more effective and visible to the general public (photo by PID/KUKL).

Table 3.2: Uses of Personal Protective Equipment in Different Work Environments

Objective	Workplace Hazard	Suggested Personal Protective Equipment
Eye and face protection	Flying particles, molten metal, liquid chemicals, gases or vapors, light radiation	Safety glasses with side shields, protective shades, etc.
 Demonstration on the use of a full set of personal protective equipment (photo by DB Singh, ADB).		 Use of personal protective equipment by project staff and workers (photo by DB Singh, ADB).
Head protection	Falling objects, inadequate height clearance, overhead power cord	Plastic helmets with top and side impact protection
Hearing protection	Noise above standard threshold (generally >70 decibels)	Hearing protectors (ear plugs or earmuffs)

Continued on next page

Table 3.2 continued

Objective	Workplace Hazard	Suggested Personal Protective Equipment
Feet protection	Falling or rolling objects, pointed objects, corrosive or hot liquids	Safety shoes and hard-sole boots for protection against moving and falling objects, liquids, and chemicals
Hand protection	Hazardous materials, cutters, hammers, vibrators, extreme temperatures	Gloves made of rubber or synthetic materials, leather, steel, insulating materials, etc.
Respiratory/eye protection	Dust, fogs, fumes, mists, gases, smokes, vapors, COVID-19 transmission, splinters	Facemasks, face shield, goggle
Body/leg protection	Extreme temperatures, hazardous materials, biological agents, cutters, nails, glass	Insulating clothing, body suits, aprons, etc. of appropriate materials, boot

Different types of barricades. Hard, green net with caution ribbon, and zinc sheet barricades are shown in these images. The barricades should be clean and neat. Avoid old corrugated galvanized iron sheets, rusted iron pipes; or torn, dirty and badly-placed green nets

(vii)   Trench shoring standards should be as per the design document.

(viii) Construction materials are not limited to cement, aggregate, rebar, scaffolding, and formwork. They may include other materials like bricks, binding wires, concrete blocks, corrugated galvanized iron (CGI) sheets, pipes, etc. Proper stockpiling of construction materials should consider the following:

a)   The pipes should be neatly piled in the stockyard or site so that they are not damaged and do not obstruct access.

b)   The fittings should be placed separately and neatly.

c)   All fittings and equipment should be placed in their delineated area as shown in the layout map with barricading.

d)   Cement and aggregate are to be covered with tarpaulin and managed neatly.

e)   Construction waste refers to any by-product of construction process that has no further uses—for example, rebar pieces, anomalous rebar members, discarded bending wires, scrap lumber, empty containers, cement bags, plastic bag, food pouches, used plastic bottles, etc. The site inspector should assess if construction waste in the site adversely affects the environment and undermines safety.

(ix)　Construction equipment includes vehicles that are directly used in construction—for example, excavators, backhoes, dump trucks, rollers, compactors, and concrete mixtures. Construction tools are any tools that have a use in construction. Some of the tools used in excavation are pickaxes, hoes, shovels, and wheelbarrows. Proper management of construction equipment and tools includes regular inspection and servicing.

(x)　Containers of used chemicals, fuel and lubricants should be kept upright with no spillage on impervious plateform. The monitor should check the hazardous chemicals and fuel spillage response mechanism.

(xi)　A spill kit is the clean-up kit used to contain, control, and clean up any leak or spill of hydrocarbons or hazardous chemicals no matter how big or small. It should include protective clothing (gloves, overalls, overshoes, safety goggles), absorbent materials (paper towels, spill pads, spill socks), disposal bags with tape or twist ties, dust pan and broom, and container for waste.

(xii)　Waste segregation bins should be available in and around labor and staff quarters, offices, site labs, storerooms, and entrances and exits of the construction site. A separate area and containers for waste deposition and recycling should be labeled with proper signage.

(xiii)　Toilets should be checked for water availability, sanitation, and connection with a septic tank (in camps) or a soak-pit (at work sites).

(xiv)　Drains refer to the wastewater conveyance system from the site. Drainage is the overall drainage system from the site. The monitor should check and grade the management of accumulated water and score the quality of wastewater management.

(xv)　A supply of at least 80 liters per day per person of nondrinking water must be maintained in the construction camp sites for toilet, bathing, and laundry purposes.

(xvi)　"Items required for Rescue" should be in place in the site during commissioning—that is, stretchers, trained first aiders, tripods (strong enough to hold a person), oxygen cylinders, whistles, and standby vehicles.

(xvii)　For proper communication between the monitoring team during commissioning, each team leader leading the monitoring team should possess a walkie talkie.

(xviii)　Good housekeeping at work sites refer to the 5S system: *Sort, Standardize, Set in Order, Sweep, and Sustain.* The site shall be kept clear of construction materials, tools, and excess soil, etc.

Chapter 4

PLANNING PHASE

23. This chapter presents a brief description of the key environmental safeguard issues that need to be addressed during the planning stage of a project. It covers environmental safeguards and mitigation as well as health and safety measures recommended in the environmental assessment documents (EIA and/or IEE) and plans (EMP, SEMP, OHS plan, quarry management plan etc.) to be considered during the work implementation.

A. Water Supply

24. The water supply and wastewater systems implemented by the PID are gravity flow type. A gravity flow system primarily contains intake, transmission pipeline, treatment plant, service reservoir, and bulk distribution. The work to be implemented by the PID will be mainly on the water supply reservoir and distribution system, bulk distribution and distribution network improvement, and wastewater sewers and treatment plant. Figure 4.1 presents the water supply-related infrastructure being implemented by the PID. The safeguard considerations related to these works in the planning phase are described in the following section.

Figure 4.1: Water Supply Pipeline Network with Service Reservoir Tank

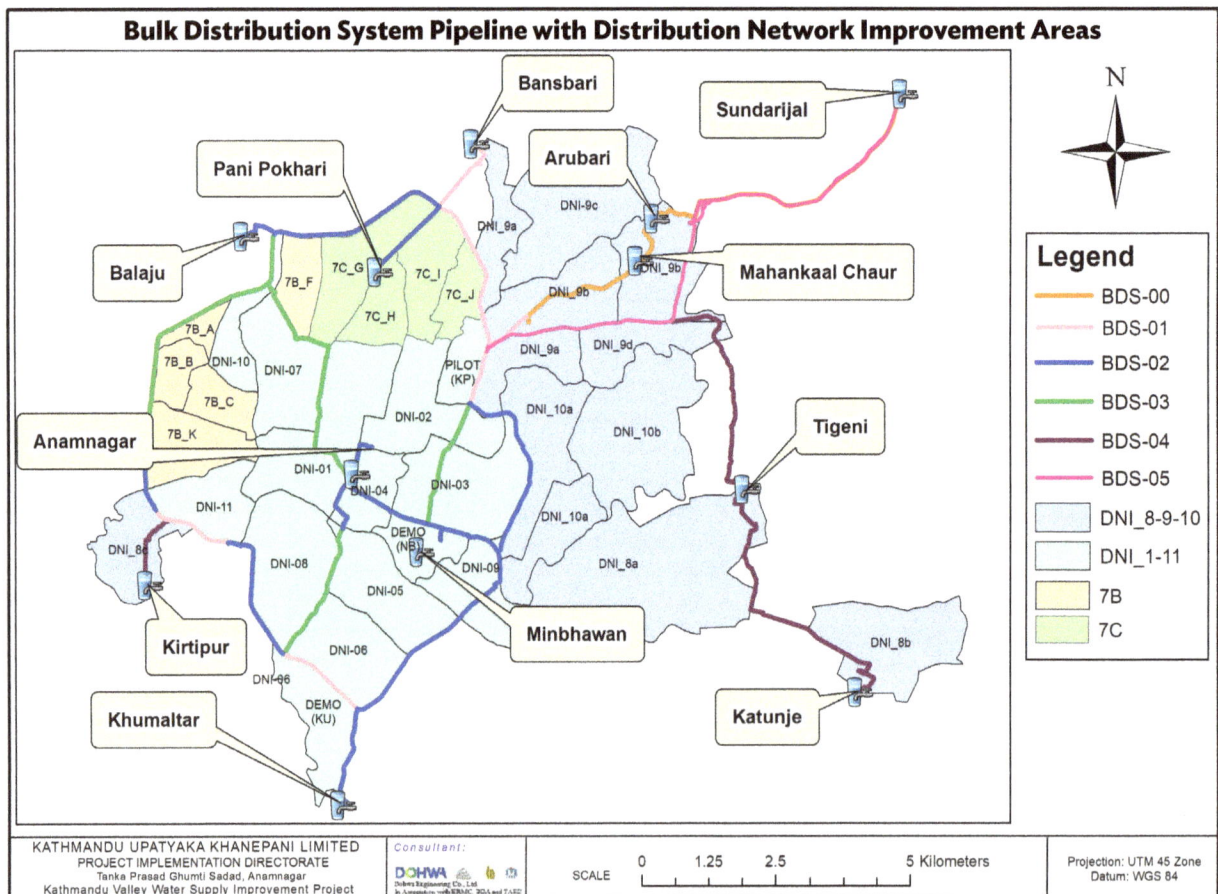

Bulk Distribution System Pipeline with Distribution Network Improvement Areas

Manual excavation of trench. The excavated soil is collected and transported to a stockpile area nearby to keep the work site free of soil and dust (photo by DB Singh, ADB).

Use of personal protective equipment in the work environment is vital in ensuring workers' safety (photo by PID/KUKL).

Service Reservoir Tank (Confined Area)

A. Environmental Impact Assessment / Initial Environmental Examination / Environmental Management Plan		
Item	**Safeguard Parameter to Consider in EMP**	**What to Ensure during Environmental Assessment ?**
Physical environment	■ Siting: lowland; area prone to flood, erosion, landslide ■ Sitemap with infrastructure details and sensitive receptors ■ Pollution management (odor, noise, air, water, vibration) ■ Adherence to the "zero soil concept" ■ Over and underground utilities and overhead transmission line ■ Drainage management ■ Temporary bypass of sewage, provision of water supply when running utilities are disturbed by the project work ■ Quarry/source of construction material ■ Use of septic tank, soak-pit, oil sump, cess pit ■ Ancient heritage sites ■ Old and vulnerable buildings and structures	■ EIA/IEE following national environmental legislations and ADB's Safeguard Policy Statement ■ Team work, identify key parameters to assess, develop checklist/questionnaire/survey forms, arrange tools and equipments, and proper preparations for collecting baseline data ■ Standard methodology for data tabulation and analysis, impact prediction, and design mitigation measures ■ Environmental management plan (EMP) prepared that also includes occupational health and safety (OHS) requirements ■ Prior government approvals listed ■ Implementation arrangement and cost for EMP/OHS plan included in bidding and contract documents Good example of a medical room with required facilities serviced by a full-time health worker (photo by DB Singh, ADB)
Biological environment	■ Critical habitat (wetland, pond, river) ■ Vegetation to be cleared ■ Landscaping and compensatory plantation ■ Terrestrial and avain fauna ■ Aquatic fauna in waterbodies	

Continued on next page

EIA / IEE / EMP from previous page continued

Item	Safeguard Parameter to Consider in EMP	What to Ensure during Environmental Assessment ?
Socioeconomic and cultural environment	■ Site office, labor camps, staff camp ■ Land and property acquisition ■ Sensitive receptors and community response ■ Heritage area, ancient structures, festival ground ■ Project–community conflict, social disturbance ■ Workers' code of conduct ■ Traffic management ■ Recreational facilities for workers	■ For workers' code of conduct, refer to Annex I (S).
Occupational health and safety (OHS)	■ OHS plan ■ Safeguard and safety officer (subject-matter expert of contractor ■ Labor insurance ■ Camp standard (structure, room, kitchen, dining, medical room, bed, window, light, fan, mosquito net, waste management, firefighting, etc. as attached with contract) ■ Supply and use of required types and quantity of personal protective equipment (PPE) ■ Medical facility and health worker ■ Work-specific safety procedure and orientation to workers including work at height, confined space, excavation, material handling, electric and fire hazard, chemical spill etc. ■ Standard operating procedures for COVID-19 risk management ■ Emergency protocol ■ Safety training Well-equipped first aid box, grievance register, and emergency phone number kept on site (photo by DB Singh, ADB).	

B. Engineering Design, Estimate, and Drawing

The EMP and OHS measures envisaged by the EIA and/or IEE should be included in the detailed design report (DPR), along with cost and institutional mechanism.

Item	EMP Requirements in Design and Cost	What to Ensure during DPR Preparation?
Structural components	Inclusion of EMP/Safety requirements in detailed design and cost. The structures may include: • Reservoir, tank, dewatering unit, pump, machine • Road, office buildings, residential buildings, laboratory • Temporary structures like labor camp, waste management site • Materials stockpile area, spoil disposal area • Landscaping and plantation	■ Ensure the EMP and safety requirements area included in the DPR with cost ■ Insert these details in Annex II–Site Inspection Form #211 A ■ Insert these details later in the SEMP/OHS plan
Others	Prepare master plan of site (on-site map) which may include: • Location of sensitive receptors • Location of air, water, and noise quality monitoring station • Location of excavation, cutting, filling • Drainage management, discharge point and type	

C. Bidding Document

What to ensure in a bidding document:

- The bidding document is screened by the safeguard expert for inclusion of the environmental management plan (EMP) requirements and to check if the EMP is attached.

- Quantifiable work items should be included in the bill of quantity (e.g., PPE, water spraying, air/water/noise monitoring, safeguard staff, health worker).

- Nonquantifiable work items could be kept under lump sum (e.g. camp, medical facility with health worker, standard operating procedure, landscaping).

- EMP compliance activity that can be envisaged only during work implementation could be kept under provisional sum.

Refer to the following items to include in bidding document, which is not an exhaustive list. On finalization of the bidding document, check that these details are included in the Annex II–Site Inspection Form #212 A, Monitoring Score Sheet #212 B, and Environment Audit Form #215 to make it project-specific.

Item	Safeguard Parameter	What to Ensure during Bid Preparation?
Environmental management plan (EMP) and occupational health and safety (OHS) compliance	■ EMP, OHS, and standard operating procedures (SOPs) for COVID-19 risk management detailed ■ Institutional mechanism for EMP and OHS assurance prepared, along with safeguard officer and safety officer (Subject-matter experts) of contractor ■ Bill of quantity (BOQ) item with cost heading for EMP and OHS compliance included ■ Required work procedure for specific type of work, such as the "zero soil" approach	The bidding document entails the following: ■ The need for a site visit before bidding to understand environmental requirements in the project and associated cost for the EMP ■ EMP and OHS (with SOP) requirements detailed in the work specification ■ Provision to mobilize full-time qualified safeguard and safety officers, and health worker ■ Specifications with cost (e.g., camp, PPE)

Continued on next page

Bidding Document from previous page continued

Item	Safeguard Parameter	What to Ensure during Bid Preparation?
EMP and OHS items to address	■ Office and camp standards ■ Work area cleanliness and safety including designated location to store pipes and construction material at site ■ Informative, safety, and traffic signboards ■ Fence and barricades ■ Work procedure for laying pipe with zero soil ■ Safety procedure before starting work inside trench, confined area, height, electric and fire hazard areas, etc ■ Arrangement for site facilities (safety PPE, safety desk, tools, drinking water, mobile toilets at sites, toilets at camp) ■ Medical facility with health worker ■ First aid at sites ■ Emergency protocol, health worker, and standby vehicle ■ Safety zones and communication system ■ Specification of hard barricade and shoring ■ Communication system ■ Plan for workers' training and awareness ■ Plan for safety of community ■ Recreational facility for workers	■ Include the EMP, OHS, and SOP parameters in the work specifications section of bidding document and in a BOQ with standards ■ For items to include in the BOQ, refer to Annex I (C) wastewater treatment plant as a sample ■ Refer to Annex I (O) for standard signboard used by the Project Implementation Directorate (PID)
Human Resource for implementation of EMP/OHS plan	■ Provision of safeguard officer, safety officer, and health worker to be appointed by contractors (subject-matter experts) ■ A system to monitor compliance with EMP using safeguard checklist with scoring of safeguard performance ■ A system to monitor compliance with OHS using OHS compliance checklist with scoring	■ Include the items in work specification of bidding document and BOQ Annex I (P) and Annex I (R) item ■ Include OHS requirements in work specification in bidding document ■ Refer to sample EMP items in BOQ in Annex I (C) ■ Refer to standard signboard used by the PID in Annex I (O)
Earmark budget for EMP/OHS plan implementation	■ Quantifiable cost ■ Unforeseeable EMP/OHS plan cost ■ Cost in BOQ to be based on EMP/Safety in EIA/IEE and not based on assumption	■ Measurable cost as BOQ item (unit rate or lump sum) ■ Unknown future cost as provisional sum ■ Include cost also in contractor's site-specific environmental management plan (SEMP)/ OHS plan

Continued on next page

Bidding Document from previous page continued

Item	Safeguard Parameter	What to Ensure during Bid Preparation?
Submissions	■ SEMP/OHS plan submission ■ EMP compliance monitoring report ■ OHS/safety compliance monitoring report ■ Grievance redress mechanism (GRM) report ■ Quarry operation plan ■ Traffic management plan ■ Workers Code of Conduct A reinforced cement concrete overhead service reservoir (photo by UWSSP, DWSS).	Inform contractor to submit EMP/OHS status report as well as prepare the following reports: ■ EMP and OHS reporting in quarterly progress report (see sample structure in Annex I (U) ■ EMP and OHS reporting in semiannual environmental monitoring report (see sample structure in Annex I (F) ■ Accident investigation report (see sample structure in Monitoring Annex II-Form #217- Accident and Injury Report). ■ GRM report (see sample table in Annex II-Form #218-#GRM). ■ Training and consultation report (as a part of monitoring reports). ■ Project completion report (environment). Refer to Annex I (F) for the project completion report, which shall include details covering the entire project period.

D. Contract Document

Please refer to the following, safeguard parameter to include in a contract document which is not an exhaustive list. Upon finalization of the contract agreement document, check that these details are included in the Annex II-Site Inspection Form #212 A, Monitoring Score Sheet #212 B, and Environment Audit Form #215 to make it project-specific.

Item	Safeguard Parameter	What to Ensure during Contract Document Preparation?

Particular conditions of the contract	■ Environmental safeguard mechanism
	■ Submission of site-specific environmental management plan (SEMP), occupational health and safety (OHS), and standard operating procedure (SOP) etc.
	■ Provision for safeguard and safety officers, and health worker of contractor
	■ Preparation of workers' code of conduct
	■ Preparation of emergency protocol
	■ Plan for pollution control and monitoring
	■ Communication, consultation, and reporting
	■ Grievance redress mechanism (GRM)
	■ Standard of environmental management plan (EMP) and OHS compliance monitoring (scoring) and penalties for noncompliance
	■ Reporting requirements
		■ Contractor to submit SEMP, OHS, and SOP plans prior to field mobilization by following project EMP (from environmental impact assessment / initial environmental examination) and others such as heritage impact assessment (HIA). Templates for SEMP, OHS, and SOP are in Form Annex I (E) and OHS guidelines of the Project Implementation Directorate (PID); the HIA structure is given in Annex I (T) and Annex II- Form #219.
		■ OHS plan shall include arrangements for personal health and safety arrangements and cover requirements for working in height, inside trenches, confined spaces, material loading and unloading, prevention of electric shock, use of barricades and barriers, and other safety procedures
		■ In the SEMP, the contractor is to submit the following:
		  ● Safeguard assurance mechanism
		  ● Staffing along with proposed biodata of environmental officer and safety officer (both subject-matter specialists for approval by Engineer)
		  ● Full-time health worker
		■ Labor camp standards (see Annex II-Labor Camp Checklist #216).
		■ Safety, traffic, and informative signboards (PID-issued standards in Annex I (O)).
		  ● Medical facility with sick bed, emergency supplies.
		  ● Proposed emergency protocol
		  ● Air, water, and noise monitoring plan (location, frequency, method)
		  ● Equipment and facilities with quality (PPE, gas detection meter, emergency evacuation equipment, other safety tools)
		■ SEMP includes joint monitoring with scoring for assessing quality of performance (see Annex II-Monitoring Score Sheet #211 B), and take corrective measures including penalty for continued noncompliance (see contract provision in Annex I (Q)).
		■ Communication and consultation plan with workers (routine) and the community (periodic).
		■ GRM and reporting (see Annex II-GRM #218).

Continued on next page

Contract Document from previous page continued

Item	Safeguard Parameter	What to Ensure during Contract Document Preparation?
Requirements and penalties	■ EMP/OHS performance scoring checklist ■ Presence of site safeguard and safety staff ■ Provision of corrective measures and penalty for noncompliance with notice to correct (NTC). See sample of NTC in Annex I (H).	■ Issue "Notice to Correct" for non-compliance to EMP/Safety requirements ■ Penalty provision based on monitoring system with scoring (refer to Annex II-Monitoring Score Sheet #211 B) and penalty clause in contract document (refer to contract provision in Annex I (Q)).
Document submission	■ SEMP template ■ OHS plan with SOPs ■ Environmental monitoring and scoring sheet (attached in SEMP) ■ Daily, weekly, monthly safeguard compliance reporting to the engineer	■ SEMP (see Annex I (E)) ■ OHS plan (see OHS guidelines of the PID) ■ SOPs for COVID-19 risk (refer to OHS guidelines of the PID) ■ Workers' code of conduct (refer to Annex I (S)) ■ Monitoring checklists ■ Reporting templates
Special requirements	■ Emerging issues in critical areas ■ Situations like COVID-19 lockdown ■ Unanticipated chance findings	■ Mention these while preparing SEMP/OHS plan. ■ Refer to these while filling in the Annex II-Environment Audit Form #215. ■ Comply with ADB's chance find procedure and HIA recommended measures

E. Site-Specific Environmental Management Plan

Item	Safeguard Parameter	What to Ensure during SEMP Preparation?
EMP/Sefety Implementation mechanism	■ Safeguard and occupational health and safety (OHS) implementation mechanism and responsibility for assurance ■ Safeguard and safety staff ■ Communication protocol ■ Monitoring system ■ Penalty mechanism ■ Reporting system	■ Overall environmental safeguard and OHS monitoring, documentation, and reporting mechanism included in the plan. ■ Environment officer and safety officer, both subject matter specialist, designated with name and areas of authority. ■ Environmental safeguard assurance checklist is included. ■ OHS assurance checklist is included. ■ Environmental safeguard scoring checklist (see Annex II-Monitoring Score Sheet #212 B) is included. ■ Reporting formats (daily, weekly, monthly). ■ Emergency protocol, health worker, and contact person in case of emergency.

Continued on next page

SEMP from previous page continued

Item	Safeguard Parameter	What to Ensure during SEMP Preparation?
Site details	▪ A site map to be prepared with planned details and nearby sensitive receptors	▪ Detailed land use map of project site showing planned structures, labor camp, engineer's office, toilets, kitchen, medical facility, fencing, stock yard, waste management, wastewater discharge point, and nearby sensitive receptors. ▪ Show batching plant, tower cranes, rebar and steel structure fabrication, workshops, laboratory. ▪ Show construction material stock yard. ▪ Sensitive receptors and location of air, water, noise level tests. ▪ Show public service utilities and overhead transmission line. ▪ Refer to Annex II–Site Inspection Form #211 A, Monitoring Score Sheet #211 B, and Stockyard Monitoring Form #212 E.
Implementation of environmental management plan (EMP) and OHS measures at particular site	▪ Mitigation measures for impact on the physical environment ▪ Mitigation measures for impact on the biological environment ▪ Mitigation measures for impact on the social and cultural environment **Examples:** ▪ Camp specification with facilities and standard ▪ Site-specific plan for safeguard and safety ▪ Signboards in required specification ▪ Medical facility and emergency protocol ▪ Reinstatement of disturbed utilities ▪ Measures for impact on the social and cultural environment ▪ Water supply by tanker and sewerage collection to compensate for disrupted services in the affected area. ▪ Zero soil procedure	▪ Included in the site-specific environmental management plan (SEMP) as listed in the EMP and if any additional issues observed at site ▪ Include these items in contractor's progress and monitoring report ▪ Refer to these while filling in the Annex II–Monitoring Score Sheet #211 B, Environment Audit Form #215, and Labor Camp Checklist #216. ▪ Refer to monitoring form for OHS compliance monitoring guidelines of the PID.
Staffing details	▪ Name and biodata of the safeguard and OHS persons ▪ Contact person in case of emergency ▪ Communication and reporting mechanism	▪ Include these in the SEMP ▪ Refer to these while filling in Annex II–Site Inspection Form #211 A and Monitoring Score Sheet #211 B.
Other Measures	▪ Pedestrian and traffic management. ▪ Inside camp human and vehicle movement plan ▪ Reinstatement of water supply line, telecom network, and electricity lines; other community infrastructures ▪ Supply of water by tanker in the water supply disturbed areas ▪ Disposal of debris and demolition wastes	▪ Refer to and ensure these while filling in Annex II–Monitoring Score Sheet #211 B, Stockyard Monitoring Form #212 E, and Environment Audit Form #215.

Bulk Distribution and Distribution Network Improvement (Linear Infrastructure)

A. Environmental Impact Assessment / Initial Environmental Examination / Environmental Management Plan

Item	Safeguard Parameter	What to Ensure during Assessment?
Physical environment	■ Alignment– lowland, flood-prone, erosion-prone ■ Basemap prepared with infrastructure details and neighboring sensitive receptors ■ Water, land, and air pollution owing to spoil, fuel and chemical leakage, and stockpiling ■ Overhead transmission line ■ Natural drainage management ■ Quarry/source of construction material ■ Trench excavation, depth, soil quality, and potential caving ■ Excavated soil management using "zero soil" concept ■ Disposal of other debris and demolition wastes ■ Dust, mud, noise, and water pollution ■ Transport and laying of pipes ■ Disposal of replaced pipes ■ Electric poles, telecom cables, optical fiber ■ Water supply lines, sewer, storm water pipe ■ Reinstatement of community facilities and services ■ Impact on old, ancient and vulnerable structures	■ Environmental impact assessment / initial environmental examination is prepared following national and policy of funding agency (ADB) ■ Proper preparations for collecting baseline data. ■ Standard methodology for data analysis, impact prediction, and design mitigation measures. ■ Detailed environmental management plan (EMP) prepared including occupational health and safety (OHS) requirements encompassing all issues listed in the Details to be Monitored (Annex I (C)). ■ Prior government approval requirements identified, listed, and planned. ■ Implementation arrangement and cost for EMP/OHS implementation included in bidding and contract documents. ■ Workers' code of conduct prepared (refer to Annex I (S)).
Biological environment	■ Critical habitat ■ Vegetation to be cleared and compensatory plantation ■ Impact on wild flora and fauna	
Socioeconomic and cultural environment	■ Site office, labor camps, staff camp ■ Land and property acquisition ■ Workers health and safety ■ Emergency protocol ■ Sensitive receptors and community response ■ Impact on heritage area, ancient structures ■ Project–community conflict, social nuisances ■ Traffic disruption in narrow lanes ■ Community safety ■ Workers' code of conduct	

Continued on next page

EIA / IEE / EMP from previous page continued

Item	Safeguard Parameter	What to Ensure during Assessment?
Occupational health and safety	■ Site-specific environmental management plan/OHS plan prepared ■ Safeguard staff of contractor provisioned ■ Workers' insurance made mandatory ■ Shoring in trenches ■ Hard barricading, green net cover around work site ■ Informative and safety signboards requirement ■ Camp facilities (room, kitchen, dining, medical room, bed, window, light, fan, mosquito net, waste management) with camp standards ■ Site camp (readymade tent, separate kitchen, toilet with soak-pit, first aid, fire extinguisher) arranged ■ PPE and proper work-specific safety arrangements ■ Standard operating procedures for COVID-19 risk management including arrangement for quarantine and isolation tents in the camps ■ Work-specific safety procedure and orientation to workers ■ Medical facility, health worker, and emergency protocol	 Standby vehicle for temporary shifting of excavated soil at site so as to keep work area free a soil and dust (photo by PID/KUKL).

Basic standard of a labor camp established by contractor in a PID contract. (photo by PID/KUKL).

Basic standard of a labor camp. (photo by PID/KUKL).

B. Engineering Design, Estimate, and Drawing

The EMP and OHS measures envisaged by the EIA and IEE should be included in the detailed design report, along with cost and institutional mechanism.

Item	Design Parameter	What to Ensure in Design and Drawing?
Pipe specifications	■ Size, type ■ Length and weight per piece ■ Joint type ■ Valve, valve chambers	■ List the type of structure in the Annex II-Site Inspection Form #212 A. ■ Include in the site-specific environmental management plan.
Trench design	■ Width, depth (Figure 4.2 presents a sample drawing of a manhole with dimensions) ■ Shoring ■ Haulage distance ■ Spoil disposal sites, quarry, and borrow pits ■ Backfilling ■ Surfacing	■ Insert these details in the Annex II-Site Inspection Form #212 A. ■ Refer to specifications and drawings in bid document and detailed design report ■ Include in the , Stockyard Monitoring Form #212 E, and Environment Audit Form #215.
Others	■ Pipe stockyard ■ Land use, access road ■ Sensitive receptors ■ Reinstatement of facilities and services	■ Insert these details in the Annex II-Site Inspection Form #212 A. ■ Insert these details in the Annex II-Monitoring Score Sheet #212 B and Environment Audit Form #215.

Figure 4.2: Sample Drawing of a Manhole

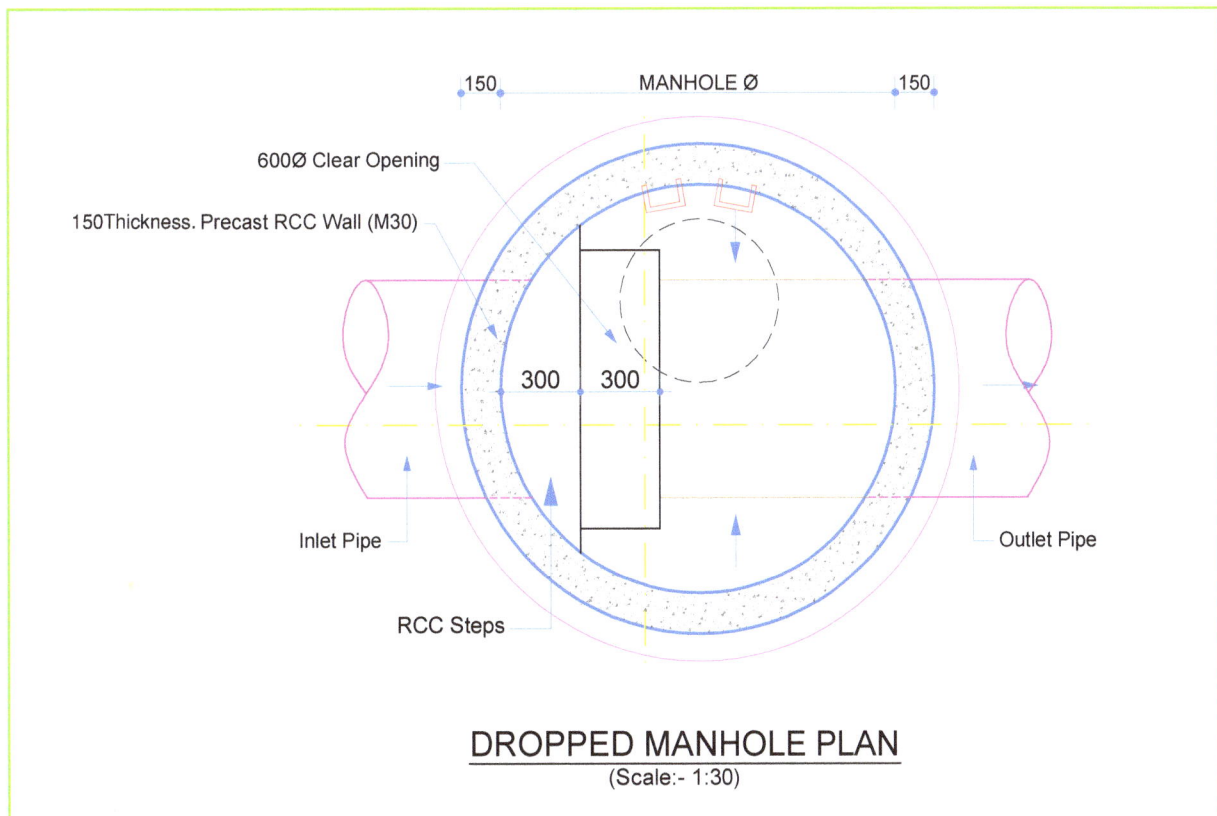

| 150 | MANHOLE Ø | 150 |

600Ø Clear Opening

150Thickness. Precast RCC Wall (M30)

300 | 300

Inlet Pipe

Outlet Pipe

RCC Steps

DROPPED MANHOLE PLAN
(Scale:- 1:30)

C. Bidding Document

What to ensure in a bidding document:

n Bid document is screened by the safeguard expert for environmental safeguards requirements and ensure the environmental management plan (EMP) is attached.

- Quantifiable work items should be included in the bill of quantity (e.g., PPEs, water sprinkling, air/water/noise monitoring, safeguard staff).
- Nonquantifiable work items could be kept under lump sum (e.g., camp, medical facility with health worker, SOP).
- EMP compliance activity that could be envisaged only during work implementation should be kept under provisional sum.

Please refer to the following, which is not an exhaustive list. Upon finalization of bidding document, check that these details are included in the Annex II-Site Inspection Form #212 A, Monitoring Score Sheet #212 B, and Environment Audit Form #215 to make it project-specific.

Item	Safeguard Parameter	What to Ensure during Bid Preparation?
Environmental management plan (EMP) and occupational health and safety (OHS) plan compliance	<ul><li>EMP, occupational health and safety (OHS), and standard operating procedures (SOPs) for COVID-19 risk management detailed.</li><li>Institutional mechanism for EMP assurance prepared along with need for safeguard officer and safety officer.</li><li>Bill of quantity (BOQ) item with cost heading for EMP/OHS compliance included.</li><li>Prepare required work procedure for specific type of work, such as "zero soil" approach.</li></ul>	The following are included in the bidding document:<ul><li>Site visit before bidding to understand environmental implication for the area.</li><li>Need for site visit before bidding to understand environmental requirements and associated cost for EMP.</li><li>EMP and OHS (with SOP) requirements detailed in the work specification Annex I (P) and Annex I (R).</li><li>Provision to mobilize full-time qualified safeguard and safety officers and health worker.</li><li>Specifications with cost (e.g., camp, PPE).</li></ul>
Human Resources for implementation of EMP	<ul><li>Provision of safeguard officer, safety officer, and health worker.</li><li>Monitor compliance with EMP using safeguard checklist with score.</li><li>Monitor compliance with OHS using OHS compliance checklist.</li></ul>	<ul><li>Include these items in the bidding document, contract document, and site-specific environmental management plan (SEMP)/OHS plan.</li><li>Insert details in the Annex II-Monitoring Score Sheet #212 B and Environment Audit Form #215.</li></ul>

Continued on next page

Bidding Document from previous page continued

Item	Safeguard Parameter	What to Ensure during Bid Preparation?
EMP and OHS implementation	■ Office and camp standards ■ Work area cleanliness and safety including designated location to store pipes and construction material ■ Informative, safety, and traffic signboards ■ Work procedure for laying pipe with zero soil approach ■ Specification of hard barricade and shoring ■ Safety procedure before starting work inside trench, confined area, height, electrified areas, etc. ■ Arrangement for site facilities (safety PPE, safety desk, tools, drinking water, mobile toilets at sites, toilets at camp) ■ Medical facility and health worker ■ First aid at sites ■ Emergency protocol, health worker, and standby vehicle ■ Safety zones and communication system ■ Specification of hard barricade and shoring ■ Communication system ■ Plan for workers training and awareness ■ Plan for safety of community ■ Recreational facility for workers ■ Training and awareness Typical Safety Hard Barricade	■ Include the EMP, OHS, and SOP parameters in the work specifications section of bidding document and in BOQ with standards Annex I (P) and Annex I (R). ■ Refer EMP items to include in BOQ in Annex I (C) (for wastewater treatment plant) as sample. Refer to standard signboard used by the Project Implementation Directorate (PID) in Annex I (O).
Reinstatement of utility services and temporary arrangement to arrange service during disruption period	■ Dismantling and reinstatement of road ■ Reinstatement of water supply line, telecom network, electricity lines, and optical fiber ■ Disposal of debris and demolition wastes ■ Plan for workers training and awareness	■ Include these items in the bid document, contract document, and the SEMP ■ Insert these details in the Monitoring in Annex II–Stockyard Monitoring Form #212 E.
Facilities and activities for staff and laborers	■ Engineer's site office and laborers' housing ■ Project signboard, safety signage, and other labels ■ Training and awareness to laborers and staff ■ Safety officers and standby vehicles	■ Measurable cost as BOQ item (unit rate or lump sum) ■ Unknown future cost (provisional sum)
Earmarked budget for EMP implementation	■ Quantifiable cost ■ Unforeseeable EMP cost	■ Measurable cost as BOQ item (unit rate or lump sum) ■ Unknown future cost (provisional sum)

Continued on next page

Bidding Document from previous page continued

Item	Safeguard Parameter	What to Ensure during Bid Preparation?
Report submission	<ul><li>SEMP compliance monitoring report</li><li>OHS/safety compliance monitoring report</li><li>Grievance redressal status report</li><li>Daily/Weekly/Monthly report on environmental compliance</li><li>Project completion report on environment</li></ul>	<ul><li>EMP implementation details and compliance monitoring report based on site condition vis-à-vis type of work</li><li>Safety (OHS and SOP) compliance report Annex II–Accident and Injury Report #217</li><li>Grievance registration and resolution report</li><li>Training and consultation report</li><li>Work completion report (environment)</li></ul>

D. Contract Document

Please refer to the following, which is not an exhaustive list. Upon finalization of the contract agreement document, check that these details are included in the Annex II–Site Inspection Form #212 A, Monitoring Score Sheet #212 B, and Environment Audit Form #215 to make it project-specific.

Item	Safeguard Parameter	What to Ensure during Contract Document Preparation?
Particular conditions of the contract	<ul><li>Environmental safeguard mechanism</li><li>Submission of site-specific environmental management plan (SEMP), occupational health and safety (OHS), and standard operating procedures (SOPs) for COVID-19 management</li><li>Provision for safeguard and safety officers and health worker</li><li>Preparation of workers' code of conduct</li><li>Preparation of emergency protocol</li><li>Plan for pollution monitoring</li><li>Communication, consultation, and reporting</li><li>Grievance redress mechanism (GRM)</li><li>Existing conditions of road and utilities</li><li>Trial trenches and trench stability</li><li>Communication, consultation, and reporting</li><li>Standard of environmental management plan (EMP) and financial penalties for noncompliance</li></ul>	<ul><li>Contractor to submit SEMP, OHS, and SOP plans prior to field mobilization by following project EMP (from the environmental impact assessment / initial environmental examination) and measures agreed in the heritage impact assessment (HIA). Refer to template for SEMP, OHS, and SOP in Annex I (E) and OHS guideline of the Project Implementation Directorate (PID). The chance find procedure for ancient artifacts is presented as Annex II–Form #219.</li><li>OHS plan shall include arrangements for personal health and safety and cover requirements for working at height, confined spaces, material loading and unloading, prevention of electric shock, barricade and barriers, and other work safety procedures.</li></ul> In the SEMP, the contractor is to submit the following: <ul><li>Safeguard assurance mechanism</li><li>Staffing along with proposed curriculum vitae of environmental officer and safety officer (both subject-matter specialists for approval by the Engineer)</li><li>Full-time health worker</li><li>Labor camp standards (see Annex II–Labor Camp Monitoring Checklist #216).</li><li>Safety, traffic, and informative signboards (PID-issued standards in Annex I (O))</li><li>Medical facility with sick bed, emergency supplies.</li><li>Proposed emergency protocol</li><li>Air, water, and noise level monitoring plan (location, frequency, method)</li><li>Equipment and facilities with quality (PPE, gas detection meter, emergency evacuation equipment, and other safety tools)</li><li>Include joint monitoring with scoring for quality of performance assessment (see Annex II–Monitoring Score Sheet #212 B) and penalty for noncompliance (see sample provision in Annex I (Q)) along with agreed procedure</li><li>GRM and reporting (see Annex II–GRM #218).</li></ul>

Continued on next page

Contract Document from previous page continued

Item	Safeguard Parameter	What to Ensure during Contract Document Preparation?
Staffing	■ Safeguard compliance assurance mechanism ■ List of safeguard and OHS staff of contractor ■ Health worker to operate medical facility	■ Include these in the SEMP ■ Refer to these while filling in the Annex II-Monitoring Score Sheet #212 B and Monitoring Score Sheet #212 C.
Requirements and penalties	■ EMP/OHS performance scoring checklist ■ Presence of site safeguard and safety staff ■ Provision of corrective measures and penalty for noncompliance (see sample of notice to correct in Annex I (H)).	■ Refer to these while preparing the SEMP. ■ Penalty provision based on monitoring system with scoring (see Annex II-Monitoring Score Sheet #212 B) and penalty clause in contract document (see sample in Annex I (Q))
Document submission	■ SEMP template ■ OHS plan with SOPs ■ Environmental monitoring and scoring sheet (attached in the SEMP) ■ Daily, weekly, monthly safeguard compliance reporting to the engineer ■ GRM report	■ SEMP (see Annex I (E) for structure) ■ OHS plan (see OHS guidelines of the PID) ■ SOP for COVID-19 risk (see OHS guideline of the PID for structure) ■ Workers' code of conduct (see Annex I (S)) ■ Monitoring checklists ■ Reporting templates ■ Grievance recording matrix
Special requirements	■ Emerging issues in critical areas ■ Situation like COVID-19 lockdown ■ Unanticipated chance findings	■ Refer to these while preparing the SEMP ■ Comply with HIA recommendation ■ Refer to these while filling in the Annex II-Environment Audit Form #215.

E. Site-Specific Environmental Management Plan

Item	Safeguard Parameter	What to Ensure during SEMP Preparation?
Institutional mechanism	■ Safeguard and occupational health and safety (OHS) implementation mechanism and responsibility for assurance ■ Safeguard and safety staff ■ Communication protocol ■ Monitoring system ■ Penalty mechanism ■ Reporting system	■ Overall environmental safeguard monitoring, documentation, and reporting mechanism ■ Safeguard and OHS-related staff with name ■ Environmental safeguard assurance checklist ■ OHS assurance checklist is included ■ Environmental safeguard Annex II-Monitoring Score Sheet #212 B and Stockyard Monitoring Form #212 E. ■ Reporting formats (daily, weekly, monthly) ■ Emergency protocol, health worker, and contact person in case of emergency is detailed

Continued on next page

SEMP from previous page continued

Item	Safeguard Parameter	What to Ensure during SEMP Preparation?
Preparatory work	■ Subdivide project area into sections based on land use, natural and ecological features, type of structure, type of impact, type of work, natural drainage etc. ■ Prepared environmental management plan and OHS plan for each section	■ Prepare base map showing sections, pipeline alignment, structures, labor camp, engineer's office, toilet, kitchen, medical facility, fencing ■ Document site-specific features ■ Show sensitive receptors, heritage area, and location of air and noise level test ■ Identify key impacts ■ Propose mitigation measure with details regarding cost and responsibility for each subsection
Site details	■ Prepare a land use map with planned details and nearby waterbodies and other sensitive receptors, road type, settlement areas, heritage areas, agriculture land, river crossing, etc. ■ Type of structures to be shown in the drawing Good quality of toilet in Labor Camp in a Construction Project (photo by DB Singh, ADB).	■ Detailed land use map of pipeline alignment and camp site showing planned structures, labor camp, engineer's office, toilets, kitchen, medical facility, fencing, stock yard, waste management, wastewater discharge point, and nearby sensitive receptors in and around the camp site; and land use along pipeline alignment in pipeline ■ Sensitive receptors and location of air, water, noise level tests ■ Rivers and river crossings needed ■ Show public service utilities and overhead transmission line ■ See Annex II-Site Inspection Form #212 A, Monitoring Score Sheet #212 B, and Stockyard Monitoring Checklist #212 E. Hand washing facility in a labor camp (photo by DB Singh, ADB).
Work procedure	■ Stepwise pipe laying plan with zero soil approach ■ Stepwise structural construction work ■ Stepwise pipe loading and unloading ■ Pipe stacking	■ Location of storage/management of excavated soil from trench ■ See Annex II-Site Monitoring Score Sheet #212 B, Stockyard Monitoring Checklist #212 E. ■ Pipe loading and unloading procedural guide

Continued on next page

SEMP from previous page continued

Item	Safeguard Parameter	What to Ensure during SEMP Preparation?
Implementation of environmental management plan and OHS measures at particular sites	▪ Mitigation measures for impact on the physical environment ▪ Mitigation measures for impact on the biological environment ▪ Mitigation measures for impact on the social and cultural environment **Examples:** ▪ Camp specification with facilities and standard ▪ Site-specific plan for safeguard and safety ▪ Signboards in required specification. ▪ Barricade and shoring ▪ Medical facility, PPE, first aid box, communication system, and emergency protocol ▪ Reinstatement of disturbed utilities. ▪ Water supply by tanker, sewerage collection, electricity supply in the service-disrupted area ▪ Zero soil concept ▪ Sludge management plan ▪ Tee cutting and compensatory plantation ▪ Festival, cultural and religious procession ▪ Pedestrian route	▪ Address all EMP measures in SEMP and OHS plan ▪ Include these items in contractor's checklist, and progress and monitoring report. Refer to these while filling in the Annex II-Monitoring Score Sheet #212 B, Environment Audit Form #215, and Labor Camp Checklist #216 ▪ Refer to the monitoring form for OHS compliance monitoring in the OHS guidelines of the Project Implementation Directorate (PID)
Staffing details	▪ Name and curriculum vitae of the environment officer and safety officer for employer's approval ▪ Health worker to operate medical facility ▪ Contact person in case of emergency	▪ Include these in the SEMP and OHS plan. ▪ Refer to these while filling in the Annex II-Monitoring Score Sheet #212 B and Site Inspection Form #212 A
Action plan	▪ Pedestrian and traffic management ▪ Reinstatement of water supply line, telecom network, and electricity lines ▪ Supply of water by tanker in the disturbed area ▪ Disposal of debris and demolition wastes	▪ Refer and ensure these while filling in the Annex II-Monitoring Score Sheet #212 B and Stockyard Monitoring Checklist #212 E ▪ Annex II-Environment Audit Form #215

B. Wastewater Management

25. The municipal wastewater treatment system (mainly sedimentation and oxidation) aims to remove the pollutants contained in the raw wastewater and facilitates management of by-products such as sludge and gas. The collected gas can be used to recover energy. Wastewater treatment plants are considered point facilities (confined area), whereas sewer networks are linear facility. The environmental safeguard measures for these two types of components of a wastewater system are different and need particular attention, as discussed below. Figure 4.3 shows a wastewater treatment plant service area, while Figure 4.4 demonstrates a sample layout of such plant.

Figure 4.3: Wastewater Treatment Plant Service Area

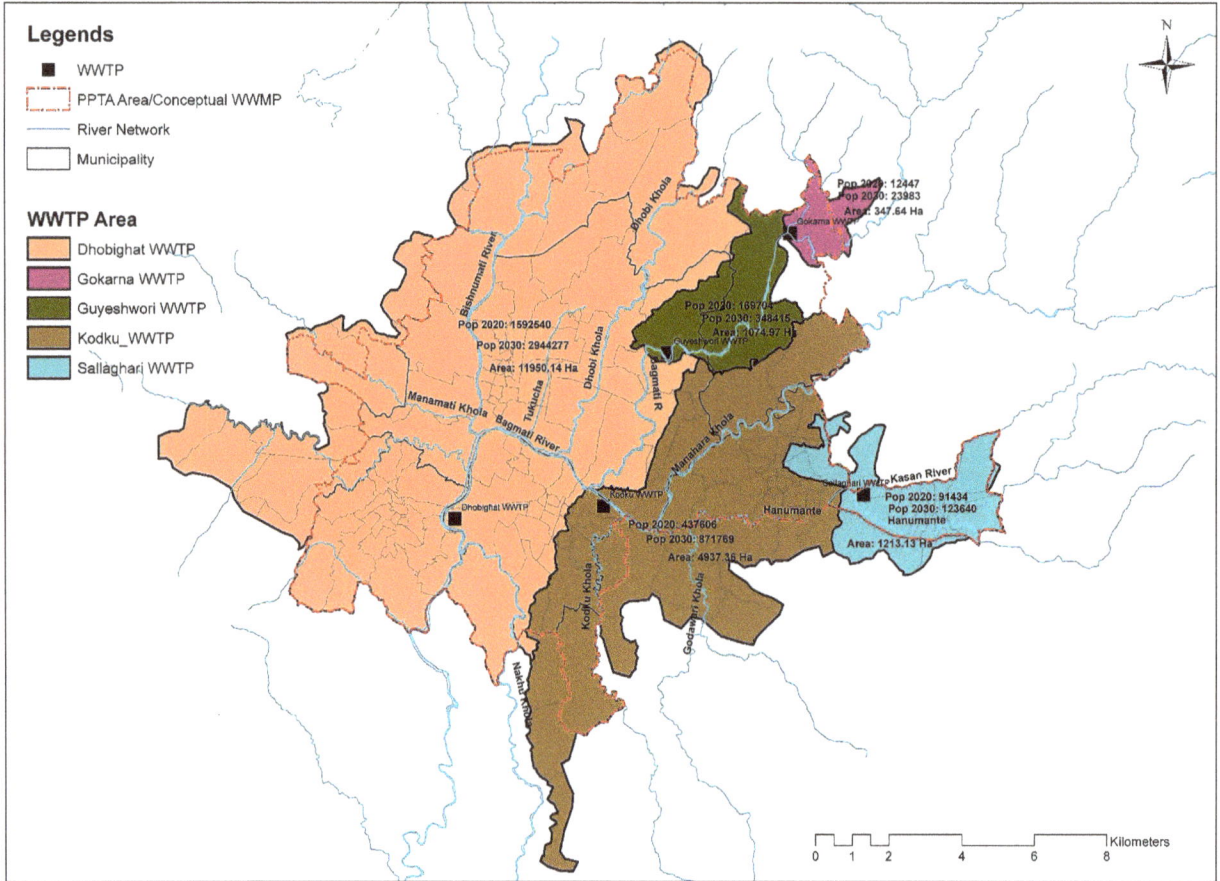

PPTA = project preparatory technical assistance, WWTP = wastewater treatment plant
Source: Project Implementation Directorate, Kathmandu Upatyaka Khanepani Limited.

Figure 4.4: Layout of a Typical Wastewater Treatment Plant

Source: Project Implementation Directorate, Kathmandu Upatyaka Khanepani Limited.

Sewer Network (Linear Structure)

	A. Environmental Impact Assessment / Initial Environmental Examination / Environmental Management Plan	
Item	**Safeguard Parameter**	**What to Ensure during Environmental Assessment?**
Physical environment	<ul><li>Alignment– lowland, flood-prone, erosion-prone</li><li>Base map prepared with infrastructure details and neighboring sensitive receptors</li><li>Water, land, and air pollution owing to spoil, fuel, stockpiling, stormwater</li><li>Overhead transmission line</li><li>Drainage management</li><li>Quarry/source of construction material</li><li>Trench excavation, depth, soil quality, and potential risk of caving</li><li>Excavated soil management using zero soil concept</li><li>Disposal of other debris and demolition wastes</li><li>Dust, mud, noise, and water pollution</li><li>Transport and laying of pipes</li><li>Disposal of replaced pipes</li><li>Electric poles, telecom cables, optical fiber</li><li>Water supply lines, sewer, stormwater pipe</li><li>Reinstatement of facilities and services</li></ul>	<ul><li>The environmental impact assessment / initial environmental examination is prepared following national environmental legislations and development partner's safeguard policy</li><li>Proper preparations for collecting baseline data at required frequency</li><li>Standard methodology for data analysis, impact prediction, and design mitigation measures</li><li>Prior government approvals requirements identified, listed, and planned</li><li>Detailed environmental management plan (EMP) prepared including occupational health and safety (OHS) requirements encompassing all issues listed in the details to be monitored (Annex I (C))</li><li>Implementation arrangement and cost for EMP/OHS implementation included in the bidding and contract documents</li><li>Follow-up for EMP measures and cost to be included in the bidding document/bill of quantity (BOQ) and condition of contract</li><li>For workers' code of conduct, refer to Annex I (S)</li></ul>
Biological environment	<ul><li>Critical habitat</li><li>Vegetation to be cleared and compensatory plantation</li></ul>	
Socioeconomic and cultural environment	<ul><li>Site office, labor camps, staff camp</li><li>Land and property acquisition</li><li>Sensitive receptors and community response</li><li>Impact on heritage area, ancient structures or chance find</li><li>Project–community conflict, social nuisances</li><li>Traffic disruption in narrow lanes</li><li>Community safety</li><li>Workers' code of conduct</li><li>Traffic management</li><li>Heritage area, festival ground</li></ul>	

Continued on next page

EIA / IEE / EMP from previous page continued

Item	Safeguard Parameter	What to Ensure during Environmental Assessment?
Occupational health and safety	■ Site-specific environmental management plan (SEMP) to be prepared along wth OHS plan ■ Safeguard staff of contractor ■ Workers' insurance ■ Shoring ■ Hard barricading, green net cover ■ Informative signboards ■ Camp facilities (readymade structure, room, kitchen, dining, medical room, bed, window, light, fan, mosquito net, toilet with septic tank, waste management) ■ Site camp (readymade tent, separate kitchen, toilet with soak-pit, first aid, fire extinguisher) ■ PPE and proper work-specific safety arrangements including safety procedure to follow during working at height, confined space, excavation, materials handling, electric and fire hazard etc. ■ Standard operating procedures (SOPs) for COVID-19 risk management including arrangement for quarantine and isolation tents in the camps ■ Safety staff of contractor ■ Medical facility, health worker, and emergency protocol	 Standard dining area in labor camp in one of the construction projects in Viet Nam (photo by DB Singh, ADB). Quality of cabins in labor camp in one of the construction projects in Viet Nam (photo by DB Singh, ADB). Modest dinning area (photo by DB Singh, ADB). Low quality kitchen in a labor camp (photo by DB Singh, ADB).

Continued on next page

B. Engineering Design, Estimate, and Drawings

The EMP and OHS measures envisaged by the EIA and/or IEE should be included in the detailed design report, along with cost and institutional mechanism.

Item	Safeguard Parameter	What to Ensure in Detail Project Report?
Pipe specifications	▪ Size, type ▪ Length and weight per piece ▪ Joint Properly stacked pipes and such area should be barricaded (photo by PID/KUKL).	▪ Insert these details in the Annex II-Site Inspection Form #213 A. ▪ Include in the site-specific environmental management plan (SEMP). ▪ Pipe for transmission line put in the stockyard.
Trench design	▪ Width, depth ▪ Shoring ▪ Haulage distance ▪ Spoil disposal sites, quarry and borrow pits ▪ Backfilling ▪ Surfacing	▪ Insert these details in the Annex II-Site Inspection Form #213 A. ▪ Refer to specifications and drawings in the bid document ▪ Include in the SEMP
Spoil and manholes	▪ Zero soil concept ▪ Spoil disposal site ▪ Disposal for broken pieces of pipes ▪ Quarry and borrow pits, if needed ▪ Manhole and cover	▪ Refer to specifications ▪ Refer to the SEMP ▪ Include in the Annex II-Monitoring Score Sheet #213 B and Environment Audit Form #215.
Others	▪ Pipe stockyard ▪ Land use, access road ▪ Sensitive receptors ▪ Reinstatement of facilities and services	▪ Refer to the SEMP ▪ Insert these details in the Annex II-Site Inspection Form #213 A. ▪ Insert these details in the Annex II-Monitoring Score Sheet #213 B and Environment Audit Form #215.

C. Bidding Document

What to ensure in a bidding document:

- The bidding document is screened by the safeguard expert for environmental and occupational health and safety (OHS) requirements and ensure if the environmental management plan (EMP) is attached to the bidding document.

- Quantifiable work items should be included in the bill of quantity (e.g., PPE, water spraying, air/water/noise monitoring, safeguard staff, health worker).

- Nonquantifiable work items could be kept under lump sum (e.g., camp, medical facility with health worker, standard operating procedure, landscaping).

- EMP compliance activity that can be envisaged only during work implementation could be kept under provisional sum.

Refer to the following, which is not an exhaustive list. On finalization of the bidding document, check that these details are included in the Annex II-Site Inspection Form #212 A, Monitoring Score Sheet #212 B, and Environment Audit Form #215 to make it project-specific.

Item	Safeguard Parameter	What to Ensure during Bid Preparation?
EMP and OHS compliance	■ Environmental management plan (EMP), occupational health and safety (OHS), and standard operating procedures (SOPs) for COVID-19 risk management detailed. ■ Institutional mechanism for EMP/safety assurance prepared, along with safeguard officer and safety officer (subject-matter expert). ■ Bill of quantity (BOQ) item with cost heading for EMP/safety compliance included ■ Required work procedure for specific type of work, such as 'zero soil' approach.	■ Need for site visit before bidding to understand environmental requirements in project and associated cost for EMP. ■ EMP and OHS (with SOP) requirements detailed in the work specification Annex I (P) and Annex I (R). ■ Provision to mobilize full-time qualified safeguard and safety officers and health worker. ■ Specifications with cost (e.g., camp, PPE)
Human resources for implementation of EMP and OHS plan	■ Provision of environment officer ■ Provision of safety officer of contractor ■ Provision of health worker ■ Provision of continued training and orientation to staff and workers ■ A system to monitor OHS plan compliance using checklist with scoring of performance quality	■ Include these items in the bidding document, contract document, and the site-specific environmental management plan (SEMP). ■ Insert these details in the Annex II-Monitoring Score Sheet #213 B, Monitoring Score Sheet #212 C, and Environment Audit Form # 215.

Continued on next page

Bidding Document from previous page continued

Item	Safeguard Parameter	What to Ensure during Bid Preparation?
EMP and OHS items to address	<ul><li>Office and camp standards</li><li>Work area cleanliness and safety including designated location to store pipes and construction material at site</li><li>Informative, safety, and traffic signboards</li><li>Fence and barricades</li><li>Work procedure for laying pipe with zero soil approach</li><li>Safety procedure before starting work inside trench, confined area, height, electrified areas, etc.</li><li>Arrangement for site facilities (safety PPE, safety desk, tools, drinking water, mobile toilets at sites, toilets at camp)</li><li>Medical facility with health worker</li><li>First aid at sites/camp</li><li>Emergency protocol, health worker, and standby vehicle</li><li>Safety zones and communication system</li><li>Specification of hard barricade and shoring</li><li>Communication system</li><li>Plan for workers' training and awareness</li><li>Plan for safety of community</li><li>Informative and safety signboards</li></ul>	<ul><li>Include the items in the work specification of bidding document and as BOQ items Annex I (P) and Annex I (R).</li><li>Include EMP/OHS requirements in the work specification in bidding document. Refer to sample EMP items in BOQ in Annex I (C).</li><li>Refer to standard signboard used by PID by the Project Implementation Directorate (PID) in Annex I (O).</li></ul>
Reinstatement of utilities services and temporary arrangement to compensate services during disruption period	<ul><li>Dismantling and reinstatement of road and walkways</li><li>Reinstatement of water supply line, telecom network, electricity lines, and optical fiber</li><li>Removal of debris and demolition waste, and broken pipe wastes</li><li>Plan for workers training and awareness</li><li>Arrangements for continuing utility service through alternative source until they are reinstated</li></ul>	<ul><li>Include these items in the bidding document, contract document, and the SEMP/OHS plan.</li><li>Insert these details in the Annex II-Stockyard Monitoring Form #212 E.</li></ul>
Facilities and activities for staff and laborers	<ul><li>Engineer's site office and labor camp</li><li>Project signboard, safety signage, and other labels</li><li>Training and awareness to laborers and staff</li><li>Safety officers and standby vehicles</li><li>Medical room and health worker</li><li>First aid kit/fire extinguishers</li></ul>	<ul><li>Include these items in the bidding document, contract document, and the SEMP/OHS plan.</li><li>Insert in the Annex II-Monitoring Score Sheet #213 B, Monitoring Score Sheet #212 C, Stockyard Monitoring Form #212 E, and Environment Audit Form #215.</li></ul>

Continued on next page

Bidding Document *from previous page continued*

Item	Safeguard Parameter	What to Ensure during Bid Preparation?
Earmark budget for EMP/OHS implementation	■ Quantifiable cost ■ Unknown EMP/OHS cost	■ Measurable cost as BOQ item (unit rate or lump sum) ■ Unknown future cost as provisional sum ■ Joint inspection/monitoring of EMP/ SEMP and OHS Plan compliance quality
Submission of reports	■ SEMP compliance monitoring report ■ OHS/safety compliance monitoring report ■ Grievance redressal status report ■ Quarterly progress report on environment ■ Contractor's daily, weekly and monthly reports on safeguard and safety ■ Project completion report on environment	■ EMP implementation details and compliance monitoring report based on site condition vis-à-vis type of work ■ Safety (OHS and SOP) compliance report ■ Accident investigation report (see Annex II-Accident Injury Report #217) ■ Grievance registration and resolution report ■ Training and consultation report ■ Work completion report (environment)

D.   Contract Document

Please refer to the following, which is not an exhaustive list. Upon finalization of the contract agreement document, check that these details are included in the Annex II-Monitoring Form #213 A, Form #213 B, and Environment Audit Form #215 to make it project-specific.

Item	Safeguard Parameter	What to Ensure during Contract Preparation?
Particular conditions of the contract	■ Environmental safeguard mechanism ■ Submission of site-specific environmental management plan (SEMP), occupational health and safety (OHS), and standard operating procedure (SOP) for COVID-19 management ■ Provision for safeguard and safety officers and health worker ■ Preparation of workers' code of conduct ■ Preparation of emergency protocol ■ Plan for pollution monitoring. ■ Communication, consultation, and reporting ■ Grievance redress mechanism (GRM) ■ Existing conditions of road and utilities ■ Trial trenches and trench stability ■ Standard of environmental management plan (EMP) and financial penalties for noncompliance	■ Contractor to submit SEMP, OHS, and SOP plans prior to field mobilization by following project EMP (from the environmental impact assessment / initial environmental examination) and measures agreed in the heritage impact assessment (HIA). Refer to the templates for SEMP, OHS, and SOP in Annex I (E) and OHS guidelines of the Project Implementation Directorate (PID). The chance find procedure for ancient artifacts is presented as Annex II-Form #219. ■ OHS plan shall include arrangements for personal health and safety and cover requirements for working in height, confined space, material loading and unloading, prevention of electric shock, and fire hazard, barricades and barriers, and other work safety procedures. In the SEMP, submit the following: ■ Safeguard assurance mechanism ■ Staffing along with proposed curriculum vitae of environmental officer and safety officer (both subject-matter specialists for approval by the Engineer) ■ Full-time health worker at medical center in the camp ■ Labor camp standards (see Annex II-Labor Camp Checklist #216).

Continued on next page

Contract Document from previous page continued

Item	Safeguard Parameter	What to Ensure during Contract Preparation?
		■ Safety, traffic, and informative signboards (PID-issued standards in Annex I (O)). ■ Medical facility with sick bed, emergency supplies. ■ Proposed emergency protocol ■ Air, water, and noise level monitoring plan (location, frequency, method) ■ Equipment and facilities with quality (PPE, gas detection meter, emergency evacuation equipment, other safety tools) ■ Include joint monitoring with scoring for assessment of quality of performance (refer to Annex II-Monitoring Score Sheet #213 B and penalty for noncompliance (refer to sample provision in Annex I (Q)) ■ GRM and reporting (refer to Annex II-GRM #218).
Staffing details	■ Safeguard compliance assurance mechanism ■ List of environment officer and safety officer of contractor ■ Health worker to operate medical facility	■ Include the staff in the SEMP ■ Refer to the staffing details while filling in the Annex II-Monitoring Score Sheet #213 B and Site Inspection Form #213 A.
Requirements and penalties	■ EMP/OHS performance scoring checklist ■ Presence of site safeguard and safety staff ■ Provision of corrective measures and penalty for noncompliance (see sample of notice to correct in Annex I (H)).	■ Refer to these while preparing SEMP ■ Penalty provision based on monitoring system with scoring. Refer to Annex II-Monitoring Score Sheet #213 B and penalty clause in contract document (see sample in Annex I (Q)).
Document submission	■ SEMP template ■ OHS plan with SOP ■ Environmental monitoring and scoring sheet (attached in the SEMP) ■ Daily, weekly, monthly safeguard compliance reporting to engineer ■ GRM report	■ SEMP (Annex I (E)) ■ OHS plan (see OHS guideline of the PID) ■ SOP for COVID-19 risk (see OHS guideline of the PID) ■ Workers' code of conduct (see #Workers Code of Conduct in Annex I (S)) ■ Monitoring checklists ■ Reporting templates ■ Grievance recording table
Special requirements	■ Emerging issues in critical areas ■ Situation like COVID-19 lockdown ■ Unanticipated and chance findings	■ Refer to these while preparing the SEMP ■ Comply with the HIA recommendations ■ Refer to these while filling in the Annex II-Environment Audit Form #215.

E. Site-Specific Environmental Management Plan

Item	Safeguard Parameter	What to Ensure during SEMP Preparation?
Institutional mechanism	■ Safeguard and occupational health and safety (OHS) implementation mechanism and responsibility for assurance ■ Safeguard and safety staff ■ Communication protocol ■ Monitoring system ■ Penalty mechanism ■ Reporting system	■ Overall environmental safeguard monitoring, documentation, and reporting mechanism ■ Safeguard and OHS staff with name ■ Environmental safeguard assurance checklist ■ OHS assurance checklist ■ Annex II–Monitoring Score Sheet #213 B and Stockyard Monitoring Form #212 E. ■ Reporting formats (daily, weekly, monthly) ■ Emergency protocol, health worker, and contact person in case of emergency
Preparatory work	■ Subdivide project area in sections based on land use, natural and ecological features, type of structure, type of impact, type of work, natural drainage, water bodies etc.	■ Prepare base map showing sections, showing pipeline alignment, structures, labor camp, engineer's office, toilet, kitchen, medical facility, fencing. ■ Document site-specific features. ■ Show sensitive receptors, heritage area and location of air and noise level test. ■ Identify key impacts. ■ Propose mitigation measure with details regarding cost and responsibility for each subsection.
Site details	■ A land use map to be prepared with planned details and nearby waterbodies and other sensitive receptors, road type, settlement areas, heritage areas, agriculture land, river crossing, etc. ■ Type of structures to be shown in drawing	■ Location of project site with clear map showing pipeline alignment and structures, labor camp, engineer's office, toilets, kitchen, medical facility, fencing, housekeeping, and other details ■ Land use, sensitive receptors, heritage area, and location of air and noise level test and mitigation measures ■ Location of storage/management of excavated soil from trench ■ See Annex II–Site Inspection Sheet #213 A, Monitoring Score Sheet #213 B, and Stockyard Monitoring Form #212 E
Work Procedure	■ Stepwise pipe laying plan with zero soil approach ■ Stepwise structural construction work ■ Stepwise pipe and other material loading and unloading	■ Location of storage/management of excavated soil from trench ■ See Annex II–Monitoring Score Sheet #213 B and Stockyard Monitoring Form #212 E ■ Pipe loading and unloading procedural guide (refer to OHS guidelines of the Project Implementation Directorate)

Continued on next page

SEMP from previous page continued

Item	Safeguard Parameter	What to Ensure during SEMP Preparation?
Implementation of the environmental management plan (EMP) and OHS measures at particular sites	■ Mitigation measures for impact on the physical environment ■ Mitigation measures for impact on the biological environment ■ Mitigation measures for impact on the social and cultural environment **Examples:** ■ Camp specification with facilities and standard ■ Site-specific plan for safeguard and safety ■ Signboards of required specification ■ Medical facility and emergency protocol ■ Reinstatement of disturbed utilities ■ Measures for impact on social and cultural environment ■ Water supply by tanker in the affected area ■ Zero soil concept ■ Sludge management plan	■ Included in the site-specific environmental management plan (SEMP) as listed in the EMP and if any additional issues observed. ■ Include these items in the contractor's progress and monitoring report. ■ Refer to these while filling in the Annex II-Monitoring Score Sheet #213 B, Monitoring Score Sheet #212 C, Environment Audit Form #215, and Labor Camp Checklist #216. Also refer to the OHS guidelines of PID.
Staffing details	■ Name and biodata of environment officer and safety officer of contractor for employers' approval ■ Health worker to operate medical facility ■ Contact person in case of emergency	■ Include the staff in the SEMP and OHS plan ■ Refer to the staffing details while filling in the Annex II-Monitoring Score Sheet #213 B and Site Inspection Form #213 A.
Action plan	■ Pedestrian and traffic management ■ Reinstatement of water supply line, telecom network, and electricity lines ■ Supply of water by tanker in the disturbed area ■ Disposal of debris and demolition wastes	■ Include these in the SEMP and OHS plan. ■ Refer to these while filling in the Annex II-Monitoring Score Sheet #213 B, Monitoring Score Sheet #212 C, Stockyard Monitoring Form #212 E, and Environment Audit Form #215.

Treatment Plant (Confined Area)

A. EIA/IEE/EMP		
Item	**Safeguard Parameter**	**What to Ensure during EIA/IEE Preparation?**
Physical environment	■ Siting: lowland; area prone to flood, erosion, landslide ■ Sitemap with infrastructure details and sensitive receptors ■ Pollution management (odor, noise, air, water, vibration) ■ Adherence with 'zero soil' concept ■ Over and underground utilities and overhead transmission line ■ Drainage management ■ Temporary bypass of sewage, provide water supply when running utilities are disturbed by the project work ■ Quarry/source of construction material ■ Use of septic tank, soak-pit, oil sump, cess pit ■ Impact on old, ancient, and vulnerable structures	■ Environmental impact assessment / initial environmental examination to be prepared following national environmental legislations and ADB funding agency's Safeguard Policy Statement ■ Proper preparations for collecting baseline data ■ Standard methodology for data analysis, impact prediction, and design mitigation measures ■ Environmental management plan (EMP) prepared that also includes occupational health and safety (OHS) requirements ■ Prior government approvals listed ■ Implementation arrangement and cost for EMP/OHS implementation included in bidding and contract documents. ■ For workers' code of conduct, refer to Annex I (S).
Biological environment	■ Critical habitat ■ Vegetation to be cleared ■ Landscaping and compensatory plantation ■ Impact on flora and fauna	
Socioeconomic and cultural environment	■ Site office, labor camps, staff camp ■ Land and property acquisition ■ Sensitive receptors and community response ■ Heritage area, ancient structures ■ Project–community conflict, social nuisances ■ Workers' code of conduct	
Occupational health and safety	■ Site-specific environmental management plan to be prepared ■ Safeguard and safety officer of contractor ■ Labor insurance ■ Camp standard (structure, room, kitchen, dining, medical room, bed, window, light, fan, mosquito net, waste management, firefighting, etc.) ■ Supply and use of PPE ■ Workers insurance ■ Medical facility and health worker ■ Work-specific safety procedure and orientation to workers ■ Standard operating procedures for COVID-19 risk management ■ Emergency protocol ■ Safety training	

B. Engineering Design, Estimate, and Drawing

Item	Safeguard Parameter	What to Ensure in Detail Project Report?

Structural components	• Master plan of site and drawings with structural dimensions should be kept ready at site. The structures may include:
	  • Reservoir, tank, digester, dewatering unit, drying bed, pump, other machines, road, office buildings, residential buildings, laboratory
	  • Temporary structures like labor camp, waste management location
	  • Material stockpile area, spoil disposal area
	  • Road, office buildings, residential buildings, laboratory, and landscaping and plantation
	  • landscaping and plantation
		• Insert these details in the Annex II-Joint Site Inspection Form #214 A, Monitoring Score Sheet #214 B, Stockyard Monitoring Form #212 E, and Environment Audit Form #215.
		• Ensure the environmental management plan (EMP) is included in the detailed design report.
		• Insert these details later in the site-specific environmental management plan (SEMP).

Others	• Site plan (on-site map) • Location of sensitive receptors • Location of air, water, and noise quality monitoring station • Location of excavation, cutting, filling • Drainage management, discharge point and type • Access road • EMP cost	• Insert these details in the Annex II-Monitoring Score Sheet #213 B, Monitoring Score Sheet #214 B, and Environment Audit Form #215.

C. Process Flow of the Plant

Item	Safeguard Parameters	What to Ensure during Process Flow Design?
Major features	• Capacity of plant, energy requirement, chemicals required	• Insert these details in the monitoring form during operations and maintenance. • Monitor during mechanical and electrical installations.
Mechanisms	• Settling, aerobic decomposition, anaerobic decomposition, mechanical dewatering, sun dry mechanism	
By-products	• Sludge and by-product (gas) management plan preparation	
Others	• Sewage outfall, pollution in receiving water and treatment options in design	

D. Bidding Document

What to ensure in a bidding document:

- The bidding document is screened by the safeguard expert for inclusion of the environmental management plan (EMP) requirements and to check if the EMP is attached.
- Quantifiable work items should be included in the bill of quantity (e.g., PPE, water sprinkling, air/water/noise monitoring, safeguard staff, health worker).
- Nonquantifiable work items could be kept under lump sum (e.g., camp, medical facility with health worker, standard operating procedure, landscaping).
- EMP compliance activity that can be envisaged only during work implementation could be kept under provisional sum.

Please refer to the following, which is not an exhaustive list. On finalization of the bidding document, check that these details are included in the Annex II–Site Inspection Form #212 A, Monitoring Score Sheet #212 B, and Environment Audit Form #215 to make it project-specific.

Item	Safeguard Parameter	What to Ensure during Bidding Document Preparation?
Environmental management plan (EMP) and OHS compliance	<ul><li>EMP, occupational health and safety (OHS), and standard operating procedures (SOPs) for COVID-19 risk management detailed</li><li>Institutional mechanism for EMP assurance prepared along with need for safeguard officer and safety officer</li><li>Bill of quantity (BOQ) item with cost heading for EMP compliance included.</li><li>Prepare required work procedure for specific type of work, such as 'zero soil' approach</li><li>Office and camps standard specifications</li><li>Work area cleanliness and safety</li><li>Project signboard, safety, and traffic signage and others</li><li>Fence and barricades</li><li>Work procedure with zero soil approach, work inside trench, confined area, height, electrified areas</li><li>Arrangement for site facilities (safety PPE, signboards, tools, drinking water, toilets)</li><li>Medical facility standard</li></ul>	Included in the bidding document:<ul><li>Need for site visit by contractor before bidding to understand environmental requirements in project and associated cost for EMP</li><li>EMP and OHS (with SOP) requirements detailed in work specification Annex I (P) and Annex I (R)</li><li>Provision to mobilize full-time qualified safeguard and safety officers and health worker</li><li>Specifications with cost (e.g., camp, PPE)</li><li>Include EMP, OHS, and SOP parameters in the "work specifications" section of the bidding document and in the BOQ Annex I (P) and Annex I (R)</li><li>Refer to EMP items to include in the BOQ in Annex I (C) (for wastewater treatment plant) as a sample</li><li>Refer to standard signboard used by the Project Implementation Directorate (PID) in Annex I (O).</li></ul>

Continued on next page

Bidding Document from previous page continued

Item	Safeguard Parameter	What to Ensure during Bidding Document Preparation?
	▪ Safety zones and communication system ▪ Specification of hard barricade and shoring ▪ Emergency protocol, health worker, and standby vehicle ▪ Communication system ▪ Plan for workers' training and awareness ▪ Plan for safety of the community ▪ Recreational facility for workers	
Execution of EMP (human resources)	▪ Provision of safeguard officer, safety officer, and health worker ▪ Monitor compliance with EMP using safeguard checklist with score ▪ Monitor compliance with OHS using OHS compliance checklist	▪ Include these items in bidding document, contract document, and the site-specific environmental management plan (SEMP). ▪ Insert details in the Annex II–Monitoring Score Sheet #214 B and Environment Audit Form #215.
Earmarked budget for EMP implementation	▪ Quantifiable cost ▪ Unforeseeable EMP cost	▪ Measurable cost as BOQ item (unit rate or lump sum) ▪ Unknown future cost as provisional sum ▪ Include in the SEMP
Submissions	▪ SEMP submission ▪ EMP compliance monitoring report. ▪ OHS/safety compliance monitoring report ▪ Grievance redress mechanism (GRM) report ▪ Daily, weekly, monthly safeguard/safety assurance reporting	Inform contractor to submit EMP/OHS status report to prepare the following: ▪ EMP and OHS reporting in the quarterly progress report (see sample structure in Annex I (U)). ▪ EMP and OHS reporting in the semiannual environmental monitoring report (see sample structure in Annex I (F)). ▪ Accident investigation report (see Annex II–Accidental Injury Report #217). ▪ Grievance registration and resolution report in Annex II–GRM #218 ▪ Training and consultation report (as part of monitoring reports) ▪ Project completion report (environment)

Continued on next page

Bidding Document from previous page continued

E. Contract Document

Please refer to the following, which is not an exhaustive list. Upon finalization of the contract agreement document, check that these details are included in the Annex II-Monitoring Form #214 A, Form #214 B, and Environment Audit Form #215 to make it project-specific.

Item	Safeguard Parameter	What to Ensure during Contract Preparation?
Particular conditions of the contract	■ Environmental safeguard mechanism. ■ Submission of site-specific environmental management plan (SEMP), occupational health and safety (OHS), and standard operating procedure (SOP) ■ Provision for safeguard and safety officers and health worker ■ Preparation of workers' code of conduct ■ Preparation of emergency protocol ■ Plan for pollution control and monitoring (air, water, noise) ■ Communication, consultation, and reporting ■ Grievance redress mechanism (GRM) ■ Standard of environmental management plan (EMP) and OHS compliance monitoring (scoring) and penalties for noncompliance Manual excavation at the heritage site of Patan Durbar Square (photo by PID/KUKL).	■ Contractor to submit SEMP, OHS, and SOP plans prior to field mobilization by following project EMP (from the environmental impact assessment / initial environmental examination) and measures agreed in the heritage impact assessment (HIA). Refer to the templates for SEMP, OHS, and SOP in Annex I (E) and OHS guideline of the Project Implementation Directorate (PID). Chance find procedure is presented as Annex II-Form #219. ■ OHS plan to include coverage for personal health and safety and requirements for working at height, confined space, material loading and unloading, prevention of electric shock, and fire hazard, barricades and barriers, and other work safety procedures. ■ In the SEMP, the contractor is to prepare a safeguard assurance mechanism and propose EMP assurance staff and safety officer (both subject-matter specialists approved by the Engineer) ■ Labor camp standards (see Annex II-Labor Camp Checklist #216) ■ Safety and informative signboards (PID-issued standards) ■ Establish medical facility with emergency supplies and service of a health worker, and emergency protocol ■ Air, water, and noise level monitoring (location, frequency, method) ■ Contractor to supply equipment and facilities with quality (PPE, gas detection meter, emergency evacuation equipment at required sites, handwashing station, and other safety preparations) ■ SEMP include joint monitoring with scoring for quality of performance assessment. Refer to Annex II-Monitoring Score Sheet #213 B, Monitoring Score Sheet 214 B, and penalty for noncompliance in Annex I (Q), along with agreed procedure for GRM and reporting
Requirements and penalties	■ EMP/OHS performance scoring checklist ■ Presence of site safeguard and safety staff ■ Provision of corrective measures and penalty for noncompliance (see sample of notice to correct in Annex I (H)).	■ Refer to these parameters while preparing the SEMP. ■ Penalty provision based on monitoring system with scoring (refer to Annex II-Monitoring Score Sheet #214 B) and penalty clause in contract document (see sample provision in Annex I (Q)). Material covered during transportation to avoid dust generation (photo by DB Singh, ADB).

Continued on next page

Contract Document from previous page continued

Item	Safeguard Parameter	What to Ensure during Contract Preparation?
Special requirements	■ Emerging issues in critical areas. ■ Situation like COVID-19 lockdown ■ Unanticipated chance findings	■ Mention these while preparing the SEMP. ■ Refer to these while filling in the Annex II-Environment Audit Form #215. ■ Comply with ADB's chance finding procedure
Document submission	■ SEMP ■ OHS plan with SOP ■ Environmental monitoring and scoring sheet (attached in the SEMP) ■ Daily, weekly, monthly safeguard compliance reporting to the engineer	■ SEMP (refer to Annex I (E)) ■ OHS plan (refer to the PID OHS guidelines) ■ SOP for COVID-19 risk (refer to the PID OHS guidelines) ■ Workers' code of conduct (refer to Annex I (S)) ■ Monitoring checklists ■ Reporting templates

A typical standard of labor camp (photos by DB Singh, ADB).

F. Site-Specific Environmental Management Plan

Item	Safeguard Parameter	What to Ensure during SEMP Preparation?
Institutional mechanism	■ Safeguard and occupational health and safety (OHS) implementation mechanism and responsibility for assurance ■ Safeguard and safety staff ■ Communication protocol ■ Monitoring system ■ Penalty mechanism ■ Reporting system	■ Overall environmental safeguard monitoring, documentation, and reporting mechanism ■ Safeguard and OHS-related staff with name and biodata ■ Environmental safeguard assurance checklist ■ Environmental safeguard (refer to the Annex II-Monitoring Score Sheet #214 B) ■ Reporting formats (daily, weekly, monthly) ■ Emergency protocol, health worker, and contact person in case of emergency

Continued on next page

SEMP from previous page continued

Item	Safeguard Parameter	What to Ensure during SEMP Preparation?
Site details	■ A site map to be prepared with planned details and nearby waterbodies and other sensitive receptors.	■ Detailed land use map of project site showing planned structures, labor camp, engineer's office, toilets, kitchen, medical facility, fencing, stock yard, waste management, wastewater discharge point, and nearby sensitive receptors. ■ Show batching plant, tower cranes, rebar and steel structure fabrication, workshops, and laboratory. ■ Sensitive receptors and location of air, water, noise level tests. ■ Refer to these while filling in the , Stockyard Monitoring Form #212 E, and Monitoring Score Sheet #214 B.
Implementation of environmental management plan (EMP) and OHS measures at particular site	■ Mitigation measures for impact on the physical environment ■ Mitigation measures for impact on the biological environment ■ Mitigation measures for impact on the social and cultural environment **Examples:** ■ Camp specification with facilities and standard ■ Site-specific plan for safeguard and safety ■ Signboards in required specification ■ Medical facility and emergency protocol ■ Reinstatement of disturbed utilities ■ Measures for impact on the social and cultural environment ■ Water supply by tanker and sewerage collection to compensate disrupted services in the affected area ■ Zero soil procedure	■ The site-specific environmental management plan (SEMP) shall include, among others, proposed sites for workers' camp, laydown areas, storage areas, and waste disposal areas; haulage routes; materials storage and handling plan; traffic management plan; specific mitigation measures; monitoring program; grievance redress mechanism (GRM); and budget. The SEMP shall be available in the language and form understandable by the worker. ■ Refer to these while filling in the Annex II-Monitoring Score Sheet #214 B, and Environment Audit Form #215. ■ Refer to the monitoring form for OHS compliance monitoring in the OHS guidelines of the Project Implementation Directorate (PID).
Staffing details	■ Name of safeguard and OHS persons of contractors ■ Contact person in case of emergency (Plans A and B)	■ Include these in the SEMP/OHS plan ■ Refer to these while filling in the Annex II-Site Inspection Form #214 A and Monitoring Score Sheet #214 B.
Action plan	■ Pedestrian and traffic management ■ Interior movement plan ■ Reinstatement of water supply line, telecom network, and electricity lines ■ Supply of water by tanker in the disturbed area ■ Disposal of debris and demolition wastes	■ Refer to and ensure these while filling in the Annex II-Monitoring Score Sheet #214 B, Monitoring Form #212 E, and Environment Audit Form #215.

Chapter 5

MONITORING AND REPORTING AT THE IMPLEMENTATION STAGE

26. This chapter describes the key considerations for environmental safeguard monitoring during the work implementation. The main purposes of monitoring are (i) to verify the effectiveness of environmental protection measures in achieving the results specified in the environmental management plan (EMP); (ii) to ensure continuous improvement through corrective measures, and that risks to the environment are not overlooked; and (iii) to collect reliable data as evidence of compliance or noncompliance so as to be able to take the agreed measures. Monitoring is an integral part of the EMP and must be traceable back to the environmental assessment.

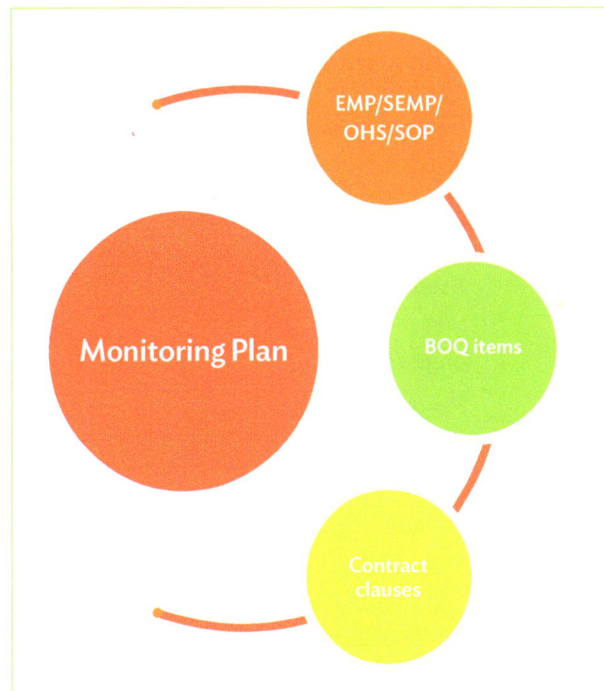

Monitoring Plan — EMP/SEMP/OHS/SOP — BOQ items — Contract clauses

27. In the project, monitoring is carried out by (i) the contractor, to assure site-specific environmental management plan (SEMP) and occupational health and safety (OHS) plan compliance; (ii) the engineer and environment experts, to ensure safeguard and safety compliance and timely corrective action; (iii) the Project Implementation Directorate (PID) to monitor the quality of performance in complying with the safeguard requirements; and (iv) third-party/external monitors, generally for projects requiring environmental impact assessment (EIA).

28. The PID, the design and supervision consultant (DSC), and the community awareness and safeguards support consultant (CASSC) should prepare a monitoring plan immediately upon approval of the SEMP and the OHS plan of the contractor. This should be based on the agreed site-specific mitigation measures detailed in the EMP or the SEMP and the OHS plan and be guided by the bill of quantity (BOQ) items and the safeguard provisions in the contract. A monitoring plan should specify (i) the monitoring methodology, (ii) the frequency and locations for sampling and data collection, (iii) the equipment to be used, and (iv) the procedures for data analysis. The monitoring could be joint between the contractor, engineer (daily, weekly, monthly), and the environment expert (monthly) or independent monitoring by the environment expert (daily, weekly, monthly). Table 5.1 presents a sample compliance monitoring plan.

Table 5.1: Sample Compliance Monitoring Plan

(to be prepared by PID based on the approved SEMP/OHS plan of contractor)

Construction Activity	Impact and Mitigation Measure	Parameter (what to measure)	Method (how)	Tools for Monitoring	Location (where)	Schedule (when)	Frequency (how many times)	Responsible (who)	Source of Funds

A. General Preparation for Structured Monitoring

29. The following stepwise preparations should be made for systematic and structured monitoring.

   (i) **Collect documents.** Gather together the EIA and/or the initial environmental examination (IEE) with the EMP; a copy of the BOQ with safeguard items; a copy of the contract with safeguard clauses; the SEMP/OHS plan; a drawing of the structure and a detailed base map/sketch (land use map) of the project implementation site with sensitive receptors, critical areas, traffic, etc. ready for reference.

   (ii) **Prepare plan.** Prepare an environmental safeguard monitoring plan based on agreed mitigation measures in the EMP, the SEMP, and the OHS plan/SOP. This could be in a matrix format. In addition, prepare a stakeholder consultation plan.

   (iii) **Prepare checklist.** Prepare an environmental compliance and OHS monitoring checklist based on the EMP (attached to the contract) and the SEMP and the OHS plan of the contractor.

   (iv) **Arrange monitoring tools.** Air, noise, and water quality monitoring should be done near sensitive receptors through the contractor. General portable equipment could be considered for in situ monitoring: (a) a real-time dust monitor (can be handheld or wall-mounted); (b) a portable decibel meter; (c) a water quality field testing kit, along with sterilized bottles for sampling; (d) a digital camera; (e) a compass and altitude meter; (f) a measuring tape; (g) global positioning system; (h) binoculars; and (i) an audio recording device (to use during interviews and consultations). If permitted, it is useful to carry a drone for an overall birds-eye view of the entire construction site. In addition, subject-matter specialists (biologists) may carry other tools and resources to count, record, and prepare samples for lab verification. The use of tools will also depend on the type and purpose of the monitoring.

   (v) **Use personal protective equipment.** All field monitoring staff must use a hardhat, a reflective jacket, safety boots, facemask or face shield, and safety gloves, and carry sanitizer while visiting the site. Use of personal protective equipment (PPE) by visiting staff will demonstrate and encourage workers with regard to the mandatory use of safety gear.

B. Water Supply System

30. Water supply projects can be categorized as either point or linear facilities. Each of these has distinct structural features, attracting specific environmental measures, such as headworks, treatment plants, and reservoirs in point facilities; and pipelines in linear facilities.

Service Reservoir Tank

Planning for Location-Wise Systematic Monitoring

31. It is recommended to adopt a per-planned and systematic procedure for monitoring a particular location within a site. An example is presented below. During the process, take as many photos and video clips as possible, and interview staff and workers for record and information verification.

Site 1. **Approach road:** What is the condition of the approach road? Is it graveled? Who maintains the road?

Site 2. **Fencing and entrance:** securely fenced, gated, guarded; quality of guard-shed; health screening; registering of all visitors with contact details; allowed to enter with/without PPE.

Site 3. **Overall condition of the site:** cleanliness (littering of empty cement bags, plastics, and construction material); drainage management and outfall; designated path for vehicle and human movement; placement of safety and informative signages and their quality and sufficiency; potholes and water pools; wild growth of shrubs and weeds; site management system in place, lighting the area; firefighting system; etc.

Site 4. **Workshop, carpentry, wielding, fabrication, and assembling areas:** flooring and roofing; drainage; electric connection; firefighting; first aid; use of PPE; communication system; lighting; waste management; work procedural manual and safety manual at site.

Site 5. **Material stockpile and storage area:** securely enclosed store sheds; chemicals and fuel stored safely over impervious surface and collector drain for accidental leakage; stockpile area at planned location shown in the base map; different construction materials as well as salvaged materials duly stockpiled and barricaded and signboard placed.

Site 6. **Labor camp:** standard of camp as per PID/contract standards; structure, roofing and flooring; room sizes; number of people living in a room; ventilation; natural light; lighting arrangements; mobile charging arrangement; fan; quality of bedding as per climatic condition; mosquito net; firefighting; first aid; code of conduct prepared and distributed; camp in-charge; kitchen; dining; water supply and reserve; wastewater in soak-pit; total number of toilets (male and female); toilet waste discharged in two-chamber septic tank.

Site 7. **Medical facility:** medical room; sick bed; saline stand; oxygen cylinder; antiseptic solution; bandage for dressing; tetanus shot; health worker; labor insurance.

Site 8. **OHS arrangement:** PPE in use and in stock; percentage of PPE use; safety signages; arrangements for working in confined spaces, at height, inside trenches; quality of electric connections and "danger" areas; firefighting facility; communication channel; arrangement that no work will be implemented without presence of site in-charge; notice to engineer; safety staff; first aid facility and medical facility on standby; workers' orientation on safeguards and safety; record of injury/accidents; cases of COVID-19 infection and management; etc.

Details for Monitoring

32. In addition to the various items to be covered during the monitoring presented above, the following details should also be monitored.

STEP 1. Preparation

Annex II-Site Inspection Form #211 A, Monitoring Score Sheet #211 B, and Environment Audit Form #215

1. Establish a routine joint site inspection schedule (say 10:30 a.m. of the first Sunday of every Nepali month). But ad hoc monitoring shall also be carried out, with independent surprise visits.
2. The engineer, the environment expert, and the contractor's safeguard and safety officers participate (mandatory).
3. The contractor will
   - Have a thematic site map on a mobile frame to refer during monitoring.
   - Keep a table of air, water, and noise monitoring ready for review.
   - Present records of the number of workers (male/female and local).
   - Present PPE type and number available at the site.
   - Ensure the site is fenced and guarded.
   - Ensure the labor camp is established as per standard.
   - Have a medical facility with a full-time health worker and emergency protocol established.
   - Have established SOP compliance arrangements.
   - Have informative and safety signages placed in the site as per requirement.
   - Have overall housekeeping plan in place.
   - Have an emergency assemblage area designated.

Routine Joint Monitoring Schedule

Location	Day	Time	Participants
XX	First Sunday of the month	XX	XX
XX	First Sunday of the month	XX	XX
XX	First Sunday of the month	XX	XX

STEP 2. Site Clearance, Excavation, Material Storage

Annex II-Site Inspection Form #211 A, Monitoring Score Sheet #211 B, and Environment Audit Form #215

1. Signage boards, direction arrows, workers and vehicular path, visitor's area designated in the site.
2. Tree and vegetation clearance (number of trees).
3. Compensatory plantation and landscaping planned and nursery planned/established.
4. Topsoil collected at designated location.
5. Excavated soil/spoil deposited at designated location or used for landscaping/reclamation.
6. Structures removed are recorded.
7. Contractor keeps thematic site maps to refer to during monitoring on a mobile frame.
8. Contractor keeps table of air, water, and noise monitoring ready for review.
9. Noise and air quality being monitored near sensitive receptors.

STEP 3. Formwork, Rebar, Concreting

Annex II-Site Inspection Form #211 A, Monitoring Score Sheet 211 B, Stockyard Monitoring Form #212 E, and Environment Audit Form #215

1. Material is covered while transporting to site.
2. Rebar, aggregates, cement bags stored at designated site duly barricaded with signboard.
3. Concrete mixture plant, tower cranes, rebar/steel, fabrication workshop in designated location with clean and tidy housekeeping.
4. Cement slurry does not flow overground and does not discharge in water body.
5. Air and noise level monitored to see if they impact on nearby sensitive receptors.
6. OHS plan/SOPs are checked to ensure arrangements are in place as per requirements.
7. Workers on rebar/steel structure using gloves, hardhats, goggles, facemasks, safety boots, safety jackets, safety belts, and full-body harnesses if working at height; ensure that the work platform at height of at least four boards (1 meter minimum) and guardrails are installed before start of work.
8. Workers doing concreting use gumboots, gloves, facemasks, hardhats, and jackets.
9. Sharp rebar pieces deposited safely at designated water recycling area.
10. Cement bags, used formworks, wastewater, and demolition waste are disposed at designated location, and the site is always kept clean of debris and waste.
11. Washing and bathing facility supplied with clean water and soap for hand washing for workers.
12. Safety supervisor present at site full-time when work is ongoing.
13. Medical facility and health worker available at camp 24x7.
14. Emergency vehicle always at standby at site.

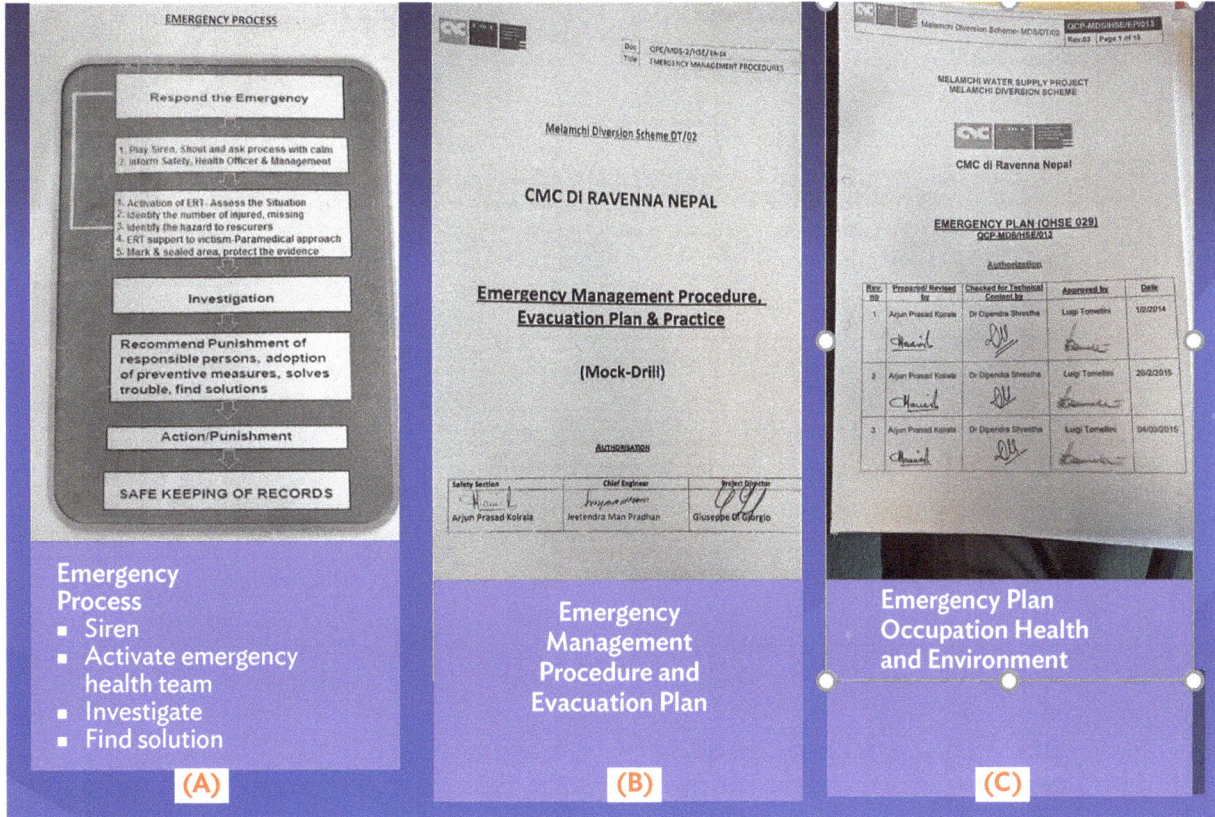

Emergency Process
- Siren
- Activate emergency health team
- Investigate
- Find solution

(A)

Emergency Management Procedure and Evacuation Plan

(B)

Emergency Plan Occupation Health and Environment

(C)

Example of safety assurance documents. The Melamchi Water Supply Project adopted safety assurance documents for emergency process (A), emergency evacuation (B), and occupational health and safety (C) (photo by DB Singh, ADB).

STEP 4. Installation of Mechanical Items, Water Testing, Landscaping

Annex II-Site Inspection Form #211 A, Monitoring Score Sheet #211 B, Stockyard Monitoring Form #212 E, and Environment Audit Form #215

Chemical spillage management kit (photo by DB Singh, ADB).

1. Ensure transport, storage, and housekeeping of mechanical items at designated place as agreed in the SEMP.
2. Ensure proper collection of packaging materials and boxes in designated place and send for recycling or disposal.
3. Monitor dust, noise, air, and water pollution and vibration from moving parts or installation of machines.
4. Ensure proper storage of chemicals.
5. Ensure landscaping of the area with plantation.

Bulk Distribution (Linear Infrastructure)

STEP 1. Site Preparation and Facilities

Annex II-Site Inspection Form #212 A, Monitoring Score Sheet #212 B, and Environment Audit Form #215

1. Prepare a procedural guide for pipe-laying with backfilling and surfacing; compliance is needed at each stage. This will also consider safety requirements while handling materials and implementing work.
2. Identify areas where land acquisition or business compensation may be needed.
3. Establish a routine joint site monitoring schedule (e.g., 10:30 a.m. of the first Sunday of every Nepali month).
4. The engineer, environment expert, and contractor's safeguard and safety officers participate in joint monitoring (mandatory).
5. The contractor will
   - Keep a pipeline alignment map on site to refer to during monitoring.
   - Keep trench drawings and dimensions with shoring, barricading, green netting, and signposts (safety, information, traffic) on site.
   - Identify the location for storing pipes.
   - Have a 'zero soil' arrangement for both wide and narrow roads for regular traffic movement.
   - Identify a location for temporary storage of soil to bring back for backfilling.
   - Keep a table of air and noise monitoring ready for review.
   - Record the number of workers (male/female and local).
   - Note the PPE used by workers on site.
   - Arrange drinking water and mobile toilets on site.
   - Follow SOPs for COVID-19 on site.
   - Give special consideration when working near sensitive receptors (schools, health posts, cultural areas, etc.).
6. The bulk distribution package will also have a camp for workers; hence, monitor that
   - The labor camp is established as per standards.
   - A medical facility with a full-time health worker and an emergency protocol are established.

A typical distribution chamber (photo by PID/KUKL).

Routine Joint Monitoring Schedule

Location	Day	Time	Participants
XX	First Sunday of the month	XX	XX
XX	First Sunday of the month	XX	XX
XX	First Sunday of the month	XX	XX

STEP 2. Supply of Pipes and Fittings, Materials

Annex II-Joint Site Inspection #212 A, Monitoring Score Sheet #212 B, Monitoring Score Sheet #212 C, Stockyard Monitoring Form #212 E, and Environment Audit Form #215

1. Plan transportation and storage of pipes and fittings prior to delivery.
2. Ensure transport, storage, and housekeeping of mechanical items in designated place as agreed in the SEMP.
3. Verify assessment of risk of pipe loading, unloading, laying, etc. as per the OHS plan.
4. Cover aggregates during transportation and plan an access route.
5. Plan to collect used cement bags, material wrappings, machine boxes, etc., for recycling or disposal.
6. Ensure proper storage and disposal of chemicals.

STEP 3. Excavation, Laying of Pipes, and Backfilling

Annex II-Joint Site Inspection #212 A, Monitoring Score Sheet #212 B, Monitoring Score Sheet #212 C, and Environment Audit Form #215

1. Excavate a trench for only one pipe length at a time following the SEMP and the procedural guide.
2. Maintain the zero soil approach and arrange a truck or wheelbarrow to directly collect and transport excavated soil depending on the width of the road.
3. Trenches that go below 1.5 meters depth must have shoring and a standard ladder (also refer to the OHS plan).
4. Trenches must be safely barricaded at critical points and covered by green net.
5. Sprinkle water on backfilled trenches at the required frequency during the dry season, and expedite resurfacing.
6. Monitor air and noise levels and if they impact on nearby sensitive receptors.
7. Check in the OHS plan/SOPs and ensure arrangements are carried out as per requirements.
8. Workers must use gloves, hardhats, facemasks, safety boots, and safety jackets.
9. Operating procedures for cranes while transporting and placing pipes and goods/material must be strictly followed, as also covered in the OHS plan.
10. Prepare a traffic diversion or management plan in consultation with traffic and the community, and give access to businesses.
11. Trenches must be backfilled within 2 days and kept safe by using hard barricades until then.
12. Prohibit the disposal of sanitary and toxic liquids, used oil, burnt lubricating oil, grease, lubricants, grouting chemicals, etc., on land and in water bodies.
13. Safety supervisor is present at site full-time when work is ongoing.
14. Medical facility and health worker must be available full time at the camp and mandatorily when the work is on-going.
15. Drinking water and mobile toilets must be arranged at the site.
16. An emergency vehicle must always be available on call and agreement signed with a nearby hospital to give prompt service in case of emergency.

STEP 4: Reinstatement of Public Utilities

Annex II-Site Inspection Form #212 A, Monitoring Score Sheet #212 B, Monitoring Score Sheet #212 C, and Environment Audit Form #215

1. Carefully remove footpath concrete blocks and stack tidily without disturbing pedestrians.
2. Machine cut and immediately remove blacktop or concrete while excavating trenches.
3. Reinstate footpath and road surfaces immediately upon completion of work for the road to not less than the original standard.
4. Make alternative arrangements for supplying utility services to houses/communities disrupted by the project work, such as sewers, water supply, electricity poles, streetlights, TV cables, etc. in consultation and agreement with the community.
5. Provide crossover platforms on trenches at regular intervals for easy access for pedestrians, residents, and shopkeepers.
6. Keep signboards at both ends of the road, giving sufficient information on the start and completion date.

C. Wastewater Management

Sewer Laying

33. Sewer laying will generally require larger-size trench excavation than laying a water supply network. Sewer-laying work should be divided into different sections while preparing the construction plan.

34. Key safeguard attributes with various activities related to sewer construction work are described below.

STEP 1. Preparation

Annex II-Site Inspection Form #213 A, Monitoring Score Sheet #213 B, and Environment Audit Form #215

1. Establish a routine joint site inspection schedule (e.g., 10:30 a.m. of the first Sunday of every Nepali month).
2. The engineer, environment expert, and contractor's safeguard and safety officers participate (mandatory).
3. Identify the area where sewer pipes will be stacked properly.
4. The contractor will
   - Keep a thematic alignment map to refer to during monitoring on a mobile frame, with sensitive receptors.
   - Keep a working drawing ready in the field.
   - Keep a table of air, water, and noise monitoring results ready for review.
   - Verify the access road and preparation of traffic plan.
   - Record project-affected entities and compensation data.
   - Clear vegetation.
   - Record the number of workers (male/female and local).
   - Record PPE type and number available on site.
   - Ensure trenches are barricaded or covered by green net as required.
   - Ensure overall housekeeping planning in place.
   - Ensure an emergency assemblage area/safety zone is designated on site where work is on land with very old and vulnerable buildings susceptible to earthquake.
5. There will also be a camp for workers. Hence, there must be:
   - Engineer's office, laboratories, and store facilities as per SEMP and PID standards.
   - A labor camp established as per SEMP and PID standards.
   - A medical facility with a full-time health worker and an emergency protocol.
   - SOP compliance arrangements.
   - Informative and safety signages in the site as per requirements.

STEP 2. Transportation of Pipes and Materials

Annex II-Site Inspection Form #213 A, Monitoring Score Sheet #213 B, Monitoring Score Sheet #212 C, Stockyard form #212 E, and Environment Audit Form #215

1. Location for pipe stockyard located and properly fenced.
2. Location for storing cement, sand, gravel, steel bars, manhole covers, pipe joining chemicals, etc. located and properly fenced.
3. Pipe transportation route between stockyard and construction site identified and coordinated with traffic.
4. Risks associated with pipe loading, unloading, laying, etc. considered and code of conduct prepared for execution as outlined in the OHS plan and the SEMP.
5. Presence of site in-charge and safety officer mandatory while conducting any construction and material handling work.
6. Construction material stockyard or warehouse with impervious floor with drainage and sump well to arrest any accidental leakage or spillage.
7. Noise and air quality monitored while transporting and handling material near sensitive receptors.

STEP 3. Excavation, Laying of Pipes, and Backfilling

Annex II–Joint Site Inspection Form #213 A, Monitoring Score Sheet #213 B, and Environment Audit Form #215

1. Excavate trench for only one pipe length at a time following the SEMP and the procedural guide.
2. Use the appropriate size of excavator and consider manual excavation at sensitive locations such as World Heritage Sites or old settlement areas.
3. Maintain a 'zero soil' approach and arrange trucks or wheelbarrows to directly collect and transport excavated soil to a designated stockpile area.
4. Trenches more than 1.5 meters depth must have shoring and a standard ladder as per the design (also refer to the OHS plan).
5. Keep shoring (to an approved standard) and dewatering pumps of a sufficient capacity and number, including spare ones in stock.
6. Sprinkle water on backfilled trenches at the required frequency during the dry season, and expedite resurfacing.
7. Prohibit the disposal of sanitary and toxic liquids, used oil, burnt lubricating oil, grease, lubricants, grouting chemicals, etc. on land and in water bodies.
8. Safely barricade trenches at critical points and cover them with green net.
9. Monitor the air and noise level and if they impact on nearby sensitive receptors.
10. Check in the OHS plans/SOPs and ensure arrangements are followed as per requirements.
11. Workers must use gloves, hardhats, facemasks, safety boots, and safety jackets.
12. Follow the SOPs for cranes for loading, unloading, and placing of pipes (also see the OHS plan).
13. Prepare a traffic diversion and management plan in consultation with traffic and the community.
14. Backfill trenches within 2 days and keep them safe using hard barricades until graveled or resurfaced.
15. Ensure a safety supervisor is present on site full-time when pipes are handled and work is ongoing.
16. Ensure a medical facility and a health worker are available at the camp at all times and there are first aid boxes at all work sites.
17. Arrange drinking water and mobile toilets on site.
18. Ensure a vehicle is always on standby at site for emergency evacuation.
19. Sign an agreement with a nearby hospital for preferential service in case of emergency.
20. Place safety and traffic information signboards at work sites.

Downloading of pipes (photo by PID/KUKL).

Figure 5.1: Cross-Section of a Typical Sewer Pipe Trench

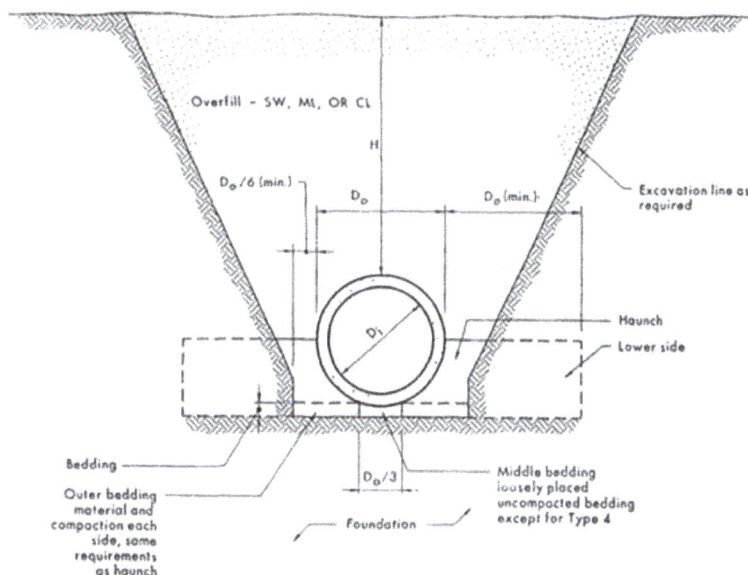

STEP 4. Reinstatement of Public Utilities

Annex II–Site Inspection Form #213 A, Monitoring Score Sheet #213 B, Monitoring Score Sheet #212 C, and Environment Audit Form #215

1. Carefully remove footpath concrete blocks and stack tidily without disturbing pedestrians. Material stock area could be covered by green net.
2. Machine cut and immediately remove blacktop or concrete from work site while excavating trenches.
3. Reinstate footpath and road surfaces immediately on completion of work in a quality not less than the original standard.
4. Make alternative arrangements for supplying utility services to houses/communities if disrupted by project work, such as sewers, water supply, electricity poles, streetlights, TV cables, landline telephones, etc. in consultation and agreement with the community.
5. Provide crossover platforms over trenches at regular intervals for easy access for pedestrians, residents, and shopkeepers and their client.
6. Keep signboards at both ends of the road/lane giving sufficient information on diversion, and start and completion dates.

Underground utilities found in an excavated trench (photo by PID/KUKL).

Wastewater Treatment Plant

STEP 1. Preparation

Annex II–Site Inspection Form #214 A, Monitoring Score Sheet #214 B, and Environment Audit Form #215

1. Establish a routine joint site inspection schedule (e.g., 10:30 a.m. of the first Sunday of every Nepali month).
2. The engineer, the environment expert, and the contractor's safeguard and safety officers participate (mandatory).
3. The contractor will
   - Keep thematic site maps along with sensitive receptors, and designs and drawings to refer to during monitoring.
   - Keep a table of air, water, and noise monitoring result ready for review.
   - Record the number of workers (male/female and local).
   - Record PPE type and number available on site.
   - Ensure the site is fenced and guarded.
   - Ensure human and vehicular movement path inside the site is designated.
   - Identify material storage and stockyard areas.
   - Ensure labor camp established as per standard and facilities like drinking water, toilet, kitchen, dining, electricity, communication, and fire extinguisher are available.
   - Ensure medical facility with full-time health worker and emergency protocol established.
   - Ensure first aid boxes are kept at all work sites.
   - Establish SOP compliance arrangements.
   - Ensure informative and safety signages placed on site as per requirement.
   - Ensure overall housekeeping planning in place.
   - Ensure emergency assemblage area designated.

Site fence, gated, and guarded (photo by PID/KUKL).

Routine Joint Monitoring Schedule

Location	Day	Time	Participants
XX	First Sunday of the month	XX	XX
XX	First Sunday of the month	XX	XX
XX	First Sunday of the month	XX	XX

STEP 2. Site Clearance, Excavation, and Material Storage

Annex II-Site Inspection Form #214 A, Monitoring Score Sheet #214 B, and Environment Audit Form #215

1. Signage boards, direction arrows, separate workers and vehicular path, and visitors area designated on site.
2. Tree and vegetation clearance (record number of trees).
3. Compensatory plantation planned and nursery established.
4. Topsoil collected at designated location for reuse dairy landscaping.
5. Excavated soil/spoil deposited at designated location or used for landscaping/ reclamation.
6. Structures removed are recorded.
7. Contractor keeps thematic site maps at site to refer to during monitoring.
8. Contractor keeps table of air, water, and noise monitoring ready for review.
9. Noise and air quality are being monitored near sensitive receptors.

Site clearance work (photo by PID/KUKL).

STEP 3. Formwork, Rebar, and Concreting

Annex II-Site Inspection Form #214 A, Monitoring Score Sheet #214 B, Stockyard Monitoring Form #212 E, and Environment Audit Form #215

1. Material is covered while being transported to site.
2. Rebar, aggregates, and cement bags are stored at designated site and duly barricaded.
3. Concrete mixture plant, tower cranes, and the rebar/steel fabrication workshop are kept at a designated location with clean and tidy housekeeping.
4. Cement slurry does not flow overground and does not discharge into water bodies.
5. Air and noise level are monitored, and check if they impact on nearby sensitive receptors.
6. Vehicles and equipment are kept well serviced and in a low emission condition.
7. OHS plan/SOP arrangements are implemented as per requirements, such as those regarding construction platforms, proper lighting, safety information, ladders, etc.
8. Workers on rebar/steel structures are using gloves, hardhats, goggles, facemasks, safety boots, safety jackets; safety belts, and full-body harnesses if working at height. Also a work platform of at least four boards (0.91 meter minimum length) and guardrail are installed before start of work while working at height.
9. Workers in concreting are using gumboots, gloves, facemasks, hardhats, and jackets.
10. Sharp rebar pieces are deposited safely at designated area for recycling.
11. Collected cement bags, used formworks, wastewater, and demolition waste are taken to designated location and the site is always kept clean of debris and waste.
12. Washing and bathing facility is supplied with clean water and soap for hand washing for workers.
13. Safety supervisor is present on site full-time when work is ongoing.
14. A medical facility and a health worker are available at the camp at all times and a first aid box is present in each key work sites and camp.
15. An emergency vehicle is always on standby at site.
16. Good housekeeping is maintained around the work area providing a respectable working environment.

Work platform at height without safety railing (photo by UWSSP/DWSS).

Laying of rebars. Use of gloves and safety boot should be mandatory (photo by PID/KUKL).

STEP 4. Installation of Mechanical Items and Landscaping

Annex II-Site Inspection Form #214 A, Monitoring Score Sheet #214 B, Stockyard Monitoring Form #212 E, and Environment Audit Form #215

1. Ensure transport, storage, and housekeeping of mechanical items at designated place and stockyard as agreed in the SEMP.
2. Ensure proper collection of packaging materials, boxes, and other waste at designated place and send for recycling or disposal.
3. Monitor dust, noise, air, and water pollution and vibration from equipment or installation of machines.
4. Ensure proper safe storage of chemicals.
5. Landscape the area through plantation by using recovered topsoil.

A typical water retaining structure (photo by PID/KUKL).

Chapter 6

OPERATION AND MAINTENANCE

35. This chapter provides a brief description of the key safeguard issues to be addressed during the Operation and Maintenance (O&M) stage.

A. Water Supply

Service Reservoir Tank

36. The key activities during O&M of the service reservoir tank include, among others, the routine and periodic cleaning of the reservoir tank, painting, checking of electromechanical equipment, handling disinfectant and chemicals, repair and replacement of valves and fittings, and overall good housekeeping around the area by maintaining landscaping, drainage, and greenery.

Bulk Distribution

37. The following are the key activities associated with the operation of the bulk distribution system:
    - Full use of the pipeline will begin after pressure testing for leakage and damage following specified norms.
    - The hydrotesting activities of the pipeline will be the responsibility of the contractor.
    - Safe disposal of the water used after testing will be a concern and should be planned prior to initiating testing.
    - Pipeline pigging[3] is performed to clean, maintain, and test new pipelines but without stopping the water flow in the pipeline in operation.
    - A routine patrol and inspection of the condition of the pipelines should be planned to enable early detection of leakage, the possibility of a natural hazard, and any damage to any new construction activity adjacent to the pipeline if special measures are not taken during construction.
    - An emergency plan should be prepared with a method statement based on the nature of the hazard or damage; the tools and equipment needed should be on standby; resources needed, including medical emergency preparation; and the team responsible for the immediate repair of damage to the pipeline owing to natural or human-caused hazards such as landslides, floods, earthquakes, and construction-related activities. The operating authorities should prepare a plan to communicate and disclose information, which should also include immediate medical and relief support to affected persons.
    - Any encroachment taking place along the right of way of the pipeline should be identified and stopped in a timely manner.
    - Transmission mains are, for the most part, located in isolated areas, such as in forests, on agricultural land, or in areas with low population density, whereas distribution lines are located in core urbanized areas with dense populations and narrow roads. Laying and operating pipelines are more complex and encounter greater challenges, including in excavation along the pipeline to install facilities such as new connections, underground cables, other water supply lines, sewer lines, roads, etc. that could damage the pipelines.

---

3   Pipeline pigging refers to the practice of using devices or implements, known as "pigs," to perform various cleaning, clearing, maintenance, inspection, dimensioning, process, and pipeline testing operations on new and existing pipelines.

B. Wastewater Management

Sewer Network

38. Excavation of the alignment for laying a sewer line and its O&M face similar environmental issues as outlined above for bulk distribution pipelines for water supply.

Wastewater Treatment Plant

39. For wastewater treatment plants, after the civil works are completed and the mechanical equipment is installed, a series of tests are conducted to move into the start-up phase. Commissioning tests of wastewater treatment plants are the operational tests conducted to ensure that the standalone units can function given the operating conditions. Performance tests are conducted to learn whether the treatment plant can function as per the standards outlined in the contract.

Precommissioning, Commissioning, and Operation

Annex II–Commissioning Monitoring Form #212 D

1. Prepare a detailed O&M manual.
2. Use the highest-quality treatment chemicals, ensure efficient use of electrical energy, and deploy well-trained staff.
3. Maintain the laboratory (required as part of the contract) and carry out routine analysis of various indexes following established frequencies.
4. Ensure input and output lines, labels, and routes are clearly visible and meet standards and specifications.
5. Ensure emergency evacuation, fire, and explosion control measures are in place.
6. Develop safety and risk assessments and operation strategies.
7. Monitor dust, noise, air, and water pollution and vibration from equipment or installation of machines.
8. Ensure proper storage and safe use of chemicals such as polymers and chlorine.
9. Ensure proper handling of sludge during treatment, dewatering, and transportation of biosolid. Give priority to the reuse of sludge as soil conditioner.
10. Monitor odor, noise, vibrations, temperature, and performance characteristics.
11. Carry out mechanical completion and integrity checking, and simulation of abnormal modes of operation.
12. Treat and disinfect the effluent.
13. Carry out laboratory testing of raw sewage and treated effluent in the plant laboratory as routine process for maintaining effluent quality requirements (as in Table 6.1).
14. Prevent odor nuisance by using oxidants such as chlorine, ozone, oxygen, potassium permanganate, etc.; spraying deodorant; or covering tanks.
15. Plan community grievance handling related to odors and other nuisance from plant operation.
16. Provide regular orientation to treatment plant operation staff. The areas to be covered during orientation are listed in Table 6.2.
17. Hold regular staff meetings to review the health and safety status of workers during O&M of the plant.

Table 6.1: Tolerance Limits for Wastewater to be Discharged into Inland Surface Water

Paramater	Value
pH	6.0–9.0
Total suspended solids	50 mg/L
BOD5	30 mg/L
Total phosphorus	2 mg/L
Total nitrogen	10 mg/:
Total coliform bacteria	400 most probable number/100 ml
Oil and grease	10 mg/L
COD	125 mg/L

BOD5 = 5-day biochemical oxygen demand, COD = chemical oxygen demand, L = liter, mg = milligram, ml = milliliter, pH = potential of hydrogen.

Source: International Finance Corporation. 2007. Environmental: Wastewater and Ambient Water Quality. In General Environmental, Health, and Safety Guidelines. Washington, DC: World Bank.

Table 6.2: Areas for Training of Operating Staff

- Technology used for sewage treatment
- Recycling and reuse of treated water
- Effective use of electricity and generation of power
- Disinfection and preparation of chemical solution of required concentration and dosage
- Details of specific treatment plant unit operations
- Maintenance schedule of all plant equipment
- Maintenance of logbook
- Preventive maintenance works to be carried out for major equipment, etc.
- Emergency protocol for accidents and out-of-control situations

Table 6.3: Hazards in Sewerage System

(1) Natural hazards

Earthquake
- Deterioration of functioning
- Floating of manholes and cave-in of roads
- Shortage of toilets

Meteorological events
- Inflow of water with a discharge over planned discharge
- Floating of manholes and scattering
- Submergence of construction sites
- Sedimentation of earth and sands in main/submain

Others
- Power blackout due to thunderstorms

(2) Human-induced hazards

Accidents
- Cave-in of road
- Malfunction of equipment
- Problems arising during operation
- Accidents at construction works
- Degradation of effluent quality
- Inflow of hazardous or noxious sewage into sewers (chemicals, oil, and radioactive materials)
- Fire hazards in the facilities

Incidents
- Outbreak of vector-transmitted disease due to sewer;
- Inflow of virus causing infectious diseases into sewer.

Inspection, Repair, and Maintenance

Annex II–Commissioning Monitoring Form #212 D

1. Prepare a minor and major maintenance and corrective repair and maintenance plan depending on the timeline (short, medium) and the condition.
2. Store spares and tools in the proper and designated location as per the master plan.
3. Safely store fuel and chemicals in an impervious shed with drainage to prevent accidental leakage or spill reaching the soil or a water body.
4. Keep sufficient safety gear (facemasks, goggles, gloves, safety boots, hardhats, safety jackets, and others as per need).
5. Prevent soil and groundwater contamination from leakage of sewage from treatment plant, and submains. Identify such leakage while monitoring visual and odor nuisances, community complaints, and regular groundwater and soil quality tests.
6. Maintain hand and face washing and bathing facilities for staff and workers so they can clean themselves after dealing with wastewater.

Pipe and valve arrangement in a wastewater treatment plant (photo by PID/KUKL).

Chapter 7

ROLES AND RESPONSIBILITIES OF STAKEHOLDERS

40. A list of the stakeholders and their responsibilities associated with water supply and wastewater project management is presented in Table 7.1. The organizational structure with the line of command is presented in Figure 7.1.

Table 7.1: Roles of Stakeholders in Environmental Safeguard Assurance

Involved Party	Responsibility	Timing	Example
Executing agency	Develops policy and strategy.	At least once a year during construction	MOWS and KUKL
	Monitors the project design, construction, and operational activities.	Every 2 years in operation stage	
Implementing agency through the PMU	Ensure EMP measures are incorporated in detailed project design and costing.	Before construction	PID
	EMP measures incorporated in bidding and contract agreement documents; key responsibility for environmental safeguard monitoring lies with the SU/PID.	Prior to contract award	Office of the Project Director and Safeguard Unit (SU) of the PID
	Acquire necessary government permits for project construction and operation.	Before and during construction	
	Ensure compensation to project-affected people and rehabilitation of community infrastructure damaged by work.	During construction	
	Ensure SEMP, OHS plan, and SOPs submitted by contractor, staff mobilized, and mitigation measures strictly implemented.	During construction and operation	
	Ensure monitoring and recordkeeping regarding environmental measures and impacts.	During construction and operation	
	Take corrective measures and impose penalty to contractors for noncompliance.	During construction	
	Community consultation and information dissemination, grievance redressal.	During construction	
	Organize orientation and training.	Full project cycle	
	Prepare and submit safeguard monitoring reports.	During construction	

Continued on next page

Table 7.1 continued

Involved Party	Responsibility	Timing	Example
Associated agencies	Liaison with implementing agency and provide approval or support shifting or reinstatement of service infrastructure.	As per need	DOR, NEA, Telecommunication, Municipality, Ward offices, NGOs, CBOs
Support consultant	Review SEMP, OHS plan, and SOPs and give approval to contractor.	During construction (before field mobilization)	DSC, CASSC, external monitors
	Support in environmental screening and assessment (IEE/DDR).	During construction	
	Prepare monitoring checklist and conduct various types of environmental safeguard compliance monitoring.	During construction	
	Provide safeguard orientation to project staff and contractor.	During construction	
	Regular supervision, issue notice to correct, and suggest corrective action to contractor or recommend penalty for noncompliance.	During construction	
	Ensure implementation of mitigation measures as per EMP, SEMP, and provisions stipulated in regular inspection reports of technical team.	During construction	
	Ensure overall stakeholder consultation and public participation and involvement in project construction as per EMP.	During construction	
	Prepare reporting template, periodic progress and monitoring reports.	During construction	
	Prepare project compilation report for the environment.	Project completion stage	

Continued on next page

Table 7.1 continued

Involved Party	Responsibility	Timing	Example
Contractors	Prepare SEMP, OHS Plan and SOP and get engineer's approval.	Immediately after contract signing and before field mobilization	
	Mobilize safeguard and safety staff.	During construction	
	Establish labor camp following PID standard and facilities as agreed in SEMP/OHS plan and contract.	During construction	
	Arrange medical facility, full-time health worker, sufficient first aid kit at workplace, and standby vehicle in case of emergency.	During construction	
	Insure workers and establish emergency protocol.	During construction	
	Implement EMP and OHS plan, and as specified in SEMP and contract.	During construction	
	Regular consultation with the local community.	During construction	
	Monitoring and recordkeeping of environmental mitigation measures as per SEMP, OHS plan, and SOPs.	During construction	
	Provide all safety measures to workers including good quality PPE, safety harnesses, communication system, gas detection meter, and evacuation equipment.	During construction	
	Implementation of corrective actions as instructed by the engineer.	During construction	
	Join engineer for routine joint SEMP and OHS plan compliance monitoring and score performance, and agree on penalty measures.	During construction	
	Record safeguard compliance and report to the engineer on daily, weekly, and monthly basis.	During construction	
Municipality, wards	Interact and support positively with project team for ensuring environmental mitigation and enhancement measures in all stages of the project.	Project period.	Concerned municipalities of Kathmandu Valley.
	Approvals in acquiring site and use of public space for work.	During construction.	
	Grievance handling and resolution.	During construction.	
NGOs, CBOs	Represent the views of project-affected people and other stakeholders for project implementation-related impacts.	During design and construction.	
	Inform on environmental and social impacts to be addressed by the project.	During construction.	
Workers	Carry out activities safely and follow work procedure, keep work area clean, and use safety gears; and follow safety rules while implementing work and residing in camps.	During construction	

Continued on next page

Table 7.1 continued

Involved Party	Responsibility	Timing	Example
Development partner (support till completion of infrastructure; operation stage monitoring responsibility will be of KUKL)	Ensure environmental assessment is carried out.	Project design and construction phase	ADB
	Consult and monitor with the PID to ensure all EMP-suggested mitigation and OHS and SOP measures are being complied.	During construction	
	Ensure corrective action plan is issued in a timely manner by the implementing agency and is being followed by the contractor.	During construction	
	Ensure stakeholder consultation and communication is being organized.	During construction	
	GRM is functional and there are no pending issues.	During construction	
	Safeguard compliance report is timely submitted.	During construction	
	Review periodic monitoring reports submitted by borrowers/clients and disclose.	During construction	

ADB = Asian Development Bank, CASSC = community awareness and safeguards support consultant, CBO = community-based organization, DDR = due diligence report, DOR = Department of Roads, DSC = design and supervision consultant, EMP = environmental management plan, GRM = grievance redress mechanism, IEE = initial environmental examination, KUKL = Kathmandu Upatyaka Khanepani Limited, MOWS = Ministry of Water Supply, NEA = Nepal Electricity Authority, NGO = nongovernment organization, OHS = occupational health and safety, PID = Project Implementation Directorate, PMU = project management unit, PPE = personal protective equipment, SEMP = site-specific environmental management plan, SOP = standard operating procedure, SU = safeguard unit.

Source: ADB.

Figure 7.1: Organizational Structure on Safeguards in the Project Implementation Directorate

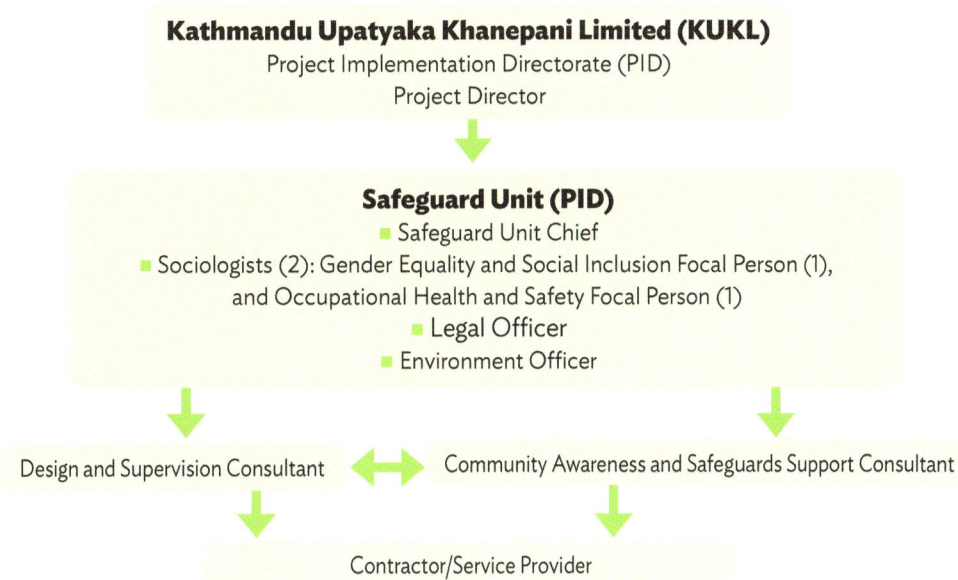

Source: Project Implementation Directorate, Kathmandu Upatyaka Khanepani Limited.

Chapter 8

REPORTING

41. Table 8.1 presents the various types of report to be prepared by the project stakeholders. An example on outline of an environmental monitoring report is given in Box 8.1.

Table 8.1: Environmental Reports to be Prepared during Construction Stage

Report	Responsibility	Frequency	Schedule	Basis of Preparation	Reviewer
Inception report	DSC CASSC	One time	30 days after mobilization	Project design, PAM, IEE/EARF, field kit	PID ADB
SEMP	Contractor	One time	30 days after contract signing	Project design, PAM, IEE/EARF, field kit, detailed site survey	DSC CASSC PID
OHS plan and SOP for COVID-19 risk management	Contractor	One time	30 days after contract signing and before field mobilization	Project design, PAM, IEE/EARF, field kit, detailed site survey	DSC PID
Daily, weekly, and monthly environmental safeguard compliance monitoring report	Contractor	Regular and routine report	As agreed with the engineer through SEMP/contract	Field documentation by contractor's safeguard officer and safety officer	DSC CASSC PID
Safeguard and safety checklist with performance scoring	Contractor DSC CASSC PID	Weekly when work is ongoing	Weekly	Joint field monitoring	PID DSC CASSC Contractor
Monthly progress report	DSC	Monthly	Monthly	Site monitoring, contract document, SEMP, OHS/SOP, field kit, joint field monitoring scoring checklists	PID
Quarterly environmental compliance monitoring report	DSC CASSC	Quarterly	Quarterly	Progress and monitoring reports of contractor, field monitoring by DSC/CASSC, joint environmental monitoring score sheet	Draft by DSC/CASSC to the PID Final by the PID to ADB
Semiannual environmental compliance monitoring report	DSC CASSC	Semiannual	15th of the next month after semiannual reporting period	Quarterly environmental compliance monitoring report, field monitoring and scoring sheet, Notice to Correct (NTC) for corrective actions, ADB mission aide memoires, grievance record, consultation programs, training	Draft by DSC/CASSC to the PID Final by the PID to ADB

Box 8.1: General Outline of an Environmental Monitoring Report

1. Introduction	**Annexes:**
2. Methodology	1. Photographs
3. Project description and progress	2. EMP/SEMP and OHS Plan with
4. Institutional arrangement for safeguard monitoring	compliance status
5. Site-specific environmental management plan compliance with comparative scoring	3. List of notices to correct issued by the engineer
6. Occupational health and safety / standard operating procedure compliance with comparative scoring	4. Air, water, noise test results
7. Compliance with follow-up action agreed with ADB mission	5. Accidents and injuries report
8. Compliance with corrective action in quarterly progress report/ semiannual environmental compliance monitoring report	6. Copy of agenda and presence in consultations
9. Compliance with project covenants	7. Grievance-related table
10. Accidents and events of activating emergency protocol	8. List of safeguard-related staff with contact number
11. Notice to Correct issued and penalty measures	
12. Stakeholder consultation	
13. Grievance redress mechanism	
14. Orientation and training	
15. Overall safeguard performance ratings	
16. Recommendation for corrective measure	

A. Air, Water, and Noise Quality Report

42. This report identifies the hotspot areas and any increase in parameters above standards as a result of construction activities. It provides a conclusion on pollution-based testing and statistical analysis of the data. The laboratory test parameters should be attached to the report. This report on test parameters shall be attached and discussed in the quarterly progress report and semiannual environmental monitoring report.

B. Site Monitoring Form and Checklist

43. Templates of site inspection forms are shown in Annex II. They are categorized as per the component and construction stages. Each template has a guidance note at the end for clarity and better understanding of the content.

Preconstruction Stage

44. Box 8.2 gives a summary of the preconstruction stage site inspection forms. These forms are to be filled by design and supervision consultant (DSC) supporting the Project Implementation Directorate (PID) during the joint site inspection with the contractor. They are to be filled only once during the preconstruction stage.

Box 8.2: Preconstruction Stage Site Inspection Forms

- Service reservoir tank Annex II-Site Inspection Form #211 A
- Bulk distribution system/distribution network improvement pipeline Annex II-Site Inspection Form #212 A
- Sewer line Annex II-Site Inspection Form #213 A
- Wastewater treatment plant –Annex II-Site Inspection Form #214 A

Construction Stage

45. For the construction stage, the environmental audit form and the stockyard monitoring form are to be filled out on a quarterly basis by the community awareness and safeguards support consultant (CASSC)/DSC/PID, mostly monitoring implementation of the EMP and OHS provisions, which are difficult to monitor on a daily basis. Box 8.3 presents a summary of the construction stage site inspection forms.

46. Templates for environmental monitoring checklists are in the Annexes. They are categorized as per the relevant components and activities. In case of any new provision in the upcoming contract packages, these checklists will be modified accordingly. Each template has a guidance note at the end for clarity and better understanding of the content. These checklists are to be filled on a daily basis by CASSC/PID/DSC. Box 8.3 summarizes the environmental safeguard compliance monitoring forms, and Box 8.4 gives the commissioning stage inspection forms.

Box 8.3: Environmental Safeguard Compliance Monitoring Forms

- Service reservoir tank Annex II-Monitoring Score Sheet #211 B
- Bulk distribution system/distribution network improvement pipeline Annex II-Monitoring Score Sheet #212 B
- Chamber/manhole/interconnection Annex II-Monitoring Score Sheet #212 C
- Sewer line Annex II-Monitoring Score Sheet #213 B
- Wastewater treatment plant Annex II-Monitoring Score Sheet #214 B

Operation and Maintenance Stage

Box 8.4: Commissioning Stage Inspection Forms

- Bulk distribution system/distribution network improvement Annex II-Commissioning Form #212 D

REFERENCES

1. Asian Development Bank (ADB). 2000. *Summary Environmental Impact Assessment of Melamchi Water Supply Project*. Kathmandu.

    _____. 2020. *Guidebook on Safeguards*. Manila.

2. Japan Water Research Center and Asian Institute of Technology. 2017. *Melamchi Water Supply Project, Kathmandu, Nepal*. Prepared for the Network on Water Technology in Asia and Pacific (NewTap) Project http://www.jwrc-net.or.jp/aswin/en/newtap/report/NewTap_IWP01.pdf.

3. *Mechanical Engineering Notes & Pipe Laying Procedures*. 2013. Procedures for Excavation, Pipe Laying, & Jointing. http://mechanicalclass.blogspot.com/2013/03/pipe-laying-procedures-excavation-and.html.

ANNEXES

ANNEX I: SAMPLE FORMS AND FORMATS

ANNEX II: MONITORING FORMS

ANNEX I: SAMPLE FORMS AND FORMATS

ANNEX I: SAMPLE FORM AND FORMATS

A.	Outline of an environmental impact assessment
B.	Outline of an initial environmental examination
C.	Example of an environmental management plan
D.	Outline of bidding document
E.	Outline of a site-specific environmental management plan
F.	Structure of a monitoring report
G.	Sample of road cut permit
H.	Sample 1 and 2 of "Notice to Correct" Letter
I.	Sample letter for organizing training to workers before commissioning
J.	Sample letter for approval of tree cutting
K.	Sample letter for compensatory tree plantation
L.	Sample letter for appointment of safeguard/safety officer
M.	Sample letter for submission of terms of reference for IEE
N.	Sample letter for compensation to the injured worker
O.	Sample of signboard standard prepared by the Project Implementation Directorate
P.	Sample of safeguard provisions in bidding document
Q.	Sample of safeguard provisions in contract
R.	Sample of safeguard provisions in bill of quantity in the bidding document
S.	Sample of workers code of conduct
T.	Outline of heritage impact assessment
U.	Structure of quarterly progress report

ANNEX I (A): OUTLINE OF AN ENVIRONMENTAL IMPACT ASSESSMENT FOR ADB CLEARANCE (TABLE OF CONTENTS)

LIST OF TABLE

LIST OF FIGURES

EXECUTIVE SUMMARY

I. INTRODUCTION
    A. Background
    B. Subproject Selection
    C. Basis and Extent of an Environmental Impact Assessment Study
    D. Objectives and Scope of the Environmental Study
    E. Relevancy of the Project

II. POLICY, LEGAL, AND ADMINISTRATIVE FRAMEWORK
    A. Nepal's Environmental Policy Framework
    B. Government of Nepal Environmental Legal Framework
    C. International Environmental Agreements
    D. Environmental Assessment Requirements of the ADB
    E. Relevant Environmental Quality and Standards

III. APPROACH AND METHODOLOGIES
    A. Literature Review
    B. Impact Area Delineation
    C. Field Study
    D. Stakeholder and Public Consultations
    E. Data Processing and Impact Identification, Prediction and Evaluation Methods
    F. Scoring of Impacts
    G. Preparation of an Environmental Impact Assessment Report and Team Members for the Environmental Impact Assessment Study

IV. DESCRIPTION OF THE PROJECT
    A. Location of the Project
    B. Type, Category, and Need of the Subproject
    C. The Subproject scope and details
    D. Sanitation Improvement
    E. Proposed Schedule for Implementation
    F. Project Requirements

V. DESCRIPTION OF THE ENVIRONMENT
    A. Physical Environment
    B. Biological Environment
    C. Socioeconomic and Cultural Environment
    D. Major Environmental Problems of Project Areas
    E. Climate Change and Adaptation

VI.   ANTICIPATED ENVIRONMENTAL IMPACTS AND MITIGATION MEASURES
   A.   Beneficial Impacts and Augmentation Measures
   B.   Adverse Impact and Mitigation Measures
   C.   Evaluation of the Impacts

VII. ANALYSIS OF ALTERNATIVES
   A.   With and Without Subproject
   B.   Subproject Location
   C.   Alternatives Related to Technology, Materials, and Implementation Procedure

VIII. ENVIRONMENTAL MANAGEMENT PLAN
   A.   Institutional Arrangement
   B.   Environmental Management Plan
   C.   Environmental Monitoring Plan
   D.   Institutional Capacity Development Plan
   E.   Staffing Requirement and Budget

IX.   INFORMATION DISCLOSURE, CONSULTATION, AND PARTICIPATION
   A.   Information Disclosure, Consultation, and Participation
   B.   Grievance Redress Mechanism

X.   MONITORING AND REPORTING

XI.   CONCLUSION AND RECOMMENDATIONS

REFERENCES

ANNEXES
1.   Rapid Environmental Assessment Checklist
2.   Environmental Standards, Sample Forms, Formats, and Report Template
   A.   Relevant Environmental Quality Standards
   B.   Sample Grievance Redress Form
   C.   Sample Traffic Management Plan
   D.   Spoil Management Plan
   E.   Sample Semiannual Environmental Monitoring Report
   F.   Sample Environmental Site Inspection Report
   G.   Reference for Plantation Cost Breakdown
3.   Schematic Layouts
4.   Integrated Biodiversity Assessment Tool Information on Biodiversity Sensitivity in Proximity of Project Area
5.   Public Consultations
6.   Survey Questionnaire
7.   Chlorine Use Guidelines
8.   Water Quality Test Results
9.   Survey Checklists
10. Consent Letters from Local Stakeholders
11. Photographs

ANNEX I (B): OUTLINE OF AN INITIAL ENVIRONMENTAL EXAMINATION FOR ADB CLEARANCE (TABLE OF CONTENTS)

LIST OF TABLE

LIST OF FIGURES

EXECUTIVE SUMMARY

I. INTRODUCTION
   A. Background
   B. Subproject Selection
   C. Basis and Extent of Initial Environmental Examination Study
   D. Objectives and Scope of the Environmental Study
   E. Relevancy of the Project

II. POLICY, LEGAL, AND ADMINISTRATIVE FRAMEWORK
   A. Nepal's Environmental Policy Framework
   B. Government of Nepal Environmental Legal Framework
   C. International Environmental Agreements
   D. Environmental Assessment Requirements of the ADB
   E. Relevant Environmental Quality and Standards

III. APPROACH AND METHODOLOGIES
   A. Literature Review
   B. Impact Area Delineation
   C. Field Study
   D. Stakeholder and Public Consultations
   E. Data Processing and Impact Identification, Prediction and Evaluation Methods
   F. Scoring of Impacts
   G. Preparation of the Initial Environmental Examination Report and Team Members for the Initial Environmental Examination Study

IV. DESCRIPTION OF THE PROJECT
   A. Location of the Project
   B. Type, Category, and Need of the Subproject
   C. The Subproject Scope and Details
   D. Sanitation Improvement
   E. Proposed Schedule for Implementation
   F. Project Requirements

V. DESCRIPTION OF THE ENVIRONMENT
   A. Physical Environment
   B. Biological Environment
   C. Socioeconomic and Cultural Environment
   D. Major Environmental Problems of Project Areas
   E. Climate Change and Adaptation

VI.   ANTICIPATED ENVIRONMENTAL IMPACTS AND MITIGATION MEASURES
A.   Beneficial Impacts and Augmentation Measures
B.   Adverse Impact and Mitigation Measures
C.   Evaluation of the Impacts

VII.   ANALYSIS OF ALTERNATIVES
A.   With and Without Subproject
B.   Subproject Location
C.   Alternatives Related to Technology, Materials, and Implementation Procedure

VIII.   ENVIRONMENTAL MANAGEMENT PLAN
A.   Institutional Arrangement
B.   Environmental Management Plan
C.   Environmental Monitoring Plan
D.   Institutional Capacity Development Plan
E.   Staffing Requirement and Budget

IX.   INFORMATION DISCLOSURE, CONSULTATION, AND PARTICIPATION
A.   Information Disclosure, Consultation, and Participation
B.   Grievance Redress Mechanism

X.   MONITORING AND REPORTING

XI.   CONCLUSION AND RECOMMENDATIONS

REFERENCES

ANNEXES
1.   Rapid Environmental Assessment Checklist
2.   Environmental Standards, Sample Forms, Formats, and Report Template
     A.   Relevant Environmental Quality Standards
     B.   Sample Grievance Redress Form
     C.   Sample Traffic Management Plan
     D.   Spoil Management Plan
     E.   Sample Semiannual Environmental Monitoring Report
     F.   Sample Environmental Site Inspection Report
     G.   Reference for Plantation Cost Breakdown
3.   Schematic Layouts
4.   Integrated Biodiversity Assessment Tool Information on Biodiversity Sensitivity in Proximity of Project Area
5.   Public Consultations
6.   Survey Questionnaire
7.   Chlorine Use Guidelines
8.   Water Quality Test Results
9.   Survey Checklists
10. Consent Letters from Local Stakeholders
11. Photographs

ANNEX I (C): A SAMPLE OF AN ENVIRONMENTAL MANAGEMENT PLAN FOR WASTEWATER TREATMENT PLANT

Activity	Impact	Mitigation Measure	Parameter to be Monitored	Method of Monitoring	Frequency	Responsibility
I. Pre-Construction Phase						
Permit and Approval	Disruptions of existing WWTP	▪ Obtain required permits and approval for disruption of existing wastewater treatment plant	▪ Ensure no disruptions to WWTP			KUKL-PID/ DSC/ CASSC
Public consultations	Social Stress	▪ Develop and implement a project communication plan	▪ Follow communications plan throughout the project ▪ Arrange to disseminate final designs, plans and activities	▪ Audit of communications plan (Audit reports); ▪ Number of meetings and participants	Monthly	KUKL-PID/ DSC/ CASSC
Workforce Camp construction	Healty living environment	▪ Establish temporary workforce camps with sanitary amenities at designated sites	▪ Camps are established at designed location with all required facilities, drainage and security	▪ Visual inspection	Monthly	KUKL-PID/ DSC/ CASSC
II. Construction Phase						
Physical Environment						
Earthwork/ topsoil stripping and excavation for trenches	Soil erosion and slope stabilization	▪ Stockpile topsoil for reuse ▪ Spoil disposal at designated sites ▪ 'Zero Soil' approach ▪ Backfill trench, temporary sealing ▪ Avoid work during the rainy days ▪ Provide proper drainage ▪ Prevent sediment flow to river	▪ Drainages systems ▪ Top soil reuse ▪ Bio-engineering measures ▪ Management of excessive spoil ▪ River water quality	▪ Site drawings with drainage system in project sites ▪ Visual inspections ▪ Logbook on spoil transportation from sites ▪ Spoil disposal area	During construction weekly	KUKL-PID/ DSC/ CASSC

Activity	Impact	Mitigation Measure	Parameter to be Monitored	Method of Monitoring	Frequency	Responsibility
Handling of waste and materials	Water/soil pollution	■ Cement slurry, chemicals do not reach waterbodies or on soil ■ Toilets with septic tanks ■ Storage of construction aggregates, hazardous materials in safe areas ■ Prohibit washing of vehicles in rivers ■ Recover used oil and lubricants and reuse or remove from the sites ■ Keep fuel, lubricant away from river/water bodies ■ Workshop/ generator on impervious floor	■ Water quality test ■ Site plan showing storage areas and receptors; ■ Prohibition/ restrictive signage ■ Oil and lubricant spill prevention measures in place ■ Presence of chemicals spillage kit	■ Physical, chemical and bacteriological test of water; ■ Distance of camp & work area from drainage ■ Toilets have septic tank; ■ Health report of workers; ■ Observation of fueling and generator areas ■ Use checklist	Once in a month	KUKL-PID/ DSC/ CASSC
Operation of machineries, vehicle and equipment	Air Pollution Dust Pollution Noise Nuisance Safety	■ Dust suppression by sprinkling water ■ Cover materials during transportation ■ Limit vehicle speed to 10–15 km/hour ■ Monitor vehicle emission ■ Regular maintenance of vehicles ■ Ventilate confined working area ■ Monitor air, water, noise level ■ Human and vehicle movement path inside camp ■ No Horn in settlement areas	■ Air quality (SOx, NOx, CO2, CO) ■ Dust (10 PM and 2.5 PM) ■ Stockpiles covered ■ Vehicle maintenance records ■ Ventilators in confined spaces ■ Community complaint for dust and noise	■ Logbook of water sprinkling ■ Photographs of stockpiles ■ Monitoring reports ■ No of ventilators ■ Feedback/ complaints from nearby residents.	Once in a month Water quality and air quality- twice a year or as required	KUKL-PID/ DSC/ CASSC

Activity	Impact	Mitigation Measure	Parameter to be Monitored	Method of Monitoring	Frequency	Responsibility
Operation of machineries, vehicle and equipment Horn honking	Noise Pollution Vibration	■ Monitor noise levels regularly at site ■ Use silencer in heavy machineries ■ Limit vehicle speed ■ Restrict power horns ■ Maintain equipment and vehicle ■ Stop crusher plants from 7:00 p.m. to 06:00 a.m. ■ Compensate for damage by vibration	■ Sound level decibel (dBA) ■ Check silencer in vehicles ■ Speed limit restrictions ■ Equipment maintenance schedule ■ Operation log of crushing plants ■ Nearby structures/ buildings	■ Sound level decibel (dBA). ■ Community complaints ■ Record of silencer in vehicle ■ Vehicles with power horns ■ Speed limit signage ■ Asset inventory for cracks in old building	Every week	KUKL-PID/ DSC/ CASSC
Construction activities and solid waste	Generation of waste	■ Store hazardous materials in safe warehouse with paved floor and drain ■ Collect, segregate and dispose construction waste at designated areas ■ Test old waste for toxicity, plan proper disposal	■ Spoil disposal area identified ■ Waste management plan prepared ■ Log of disposal of waste	■ Check waste generated and disposed ■ Waste management plan ■ Inspection of disposal areas, photographs	Bi-weekly	KUKL-PID/ DSC/ CASSC
Biological Environment						
Vegetation Clearance	Loss of green coverage	■ Compensatory and greenery promotion and plantation ■ Do not use firewood for cooking and heating	■ Use of timber and wood ■ Availability of LPG/kerosene	■ Use of LPG/ kerosene ■ Plan for compensatory plantation, nursery etc.	Monthly	KUKL-PID/ DSC/ CASSC

Activity	Impact	Mitigation Measure	Parameter to be Monitored	Method of Monitoring	Frequency	Responsibility
Cultural and Socio-economic Environment						
Work environment	Health and Safety (OHS)	■ Workers camp as per PID standard (fence, kitchen, dining, toilet, water, electricity) ■ Medical facility with a health worker ■ Regular health checkup and insurance ■ Training workers (safety, health, HIV) ■ Safety signboards ■ Use of PPE, and compensate for injuries/Accident	■ Camp standard and facility ■ Full supply in medical facility ■ Health worker insurance ■ Training program, signboards ■ Use of PPEs ■ Compensation for injuries and accidents	■ Quality of camp as per SEMP/PID standard ■ Health, accident records ■ Health worker at medical facility ■ Number of training and participants ■ Review insurance form	Daily/ Weekly	KUKL-PID/ DSC/ CASSC
Construction activities	Damage of infrastructure and community services during works	■ Reinstate damage community assets (electric pole, telephone lines, water supply pipes, sewerage lines, roads) ■ Arrange temporary service until disruption ■ Regular community consultation	■ Reinstatement of infrastructures ■ Arrangement of temporary service ■ Community consultations	■ Field observation ■ Community consultation record ■ Design & drawings ■ Consult with local people and workers	Weekly	KUKL-PID/ DSC/ CASSC
Construction activity	Traffic disruption	■ Manage traffic seeking help of and coordination with traffic police ■ Install safety and traffic signals, if required around the WWTP site ■ Operationalize GRM	■ Working schedules and traffic plans; ■ Information about construction to local people	■ Complaints from commuters ■ Availability of sufficient signboards	Weekly	KUKL-PID/ DSC/ CASSC
Construction activity	Employment to local people	■ Employ local people especially affected families and women ■ No gender biased wage rate ■ No child labor	■ Number of locals employed ■ Wage rate to male & female ■ Any cases of child labor	■ List of employees with nationality, age gender, ethnicity etc.	Monthly	KUKL-PID/ DSC/ CASSC

Activity	Impact	Mitigation Measure	Parameter to be Monitored	Method of Monitoring	Frequency	Responsibility
Outside workers in the project	Increase in social stress, crime and conflict	■ Prohibit gambling and alcohol in the camp ■ Instruct the workforce to respect the local cultures, traditions, rights ■ Provide security in contractors camp ■ Provide recreational facility in camp	■ Situation of social disharmony ■ Awareness program ■ Workers/staff code of conduct	■ Crime records and causes ■ Security situation in camps ■ Audit of workers code of conduct	Monthly	KUKL-PID/ DSC/ CASSC
Operation Phase						
Discharge of industrial wastes to WWTS	Downstream pollution, health and environmental risks	■ Train workers on OHS hazards ■ Provide PPE ■ Monitor illegal discharge of industrial wastes to the system ■ Enforce regulation	■ Training on waste management ■ Monitoring at the inlet of WWTP for electrical conductivity and dissolved oxygen	■ Visual observation ■ EC (for electrical conductivity ■ DO (mg/l)	Monthly	KUKL/ KVWSMB
Release of wastewater to river	Downstream pollution, health and environmental risks	■ Treat wastewater to meet the effluent standards before releasing in river ■ Test quality of the treated wastewater and river water	■ Quality of treated wastewater that will be released to river: total suspended solid (TSS), biological oxygen demand (BOD), and heavy metals in mg/l, pH, temperature (^0C)	■ Sampling and laboratory test	Monthly or as required	KUKL/ KVWSMB
Overflow flooding	Public and env. health hazards	■ Careful operation and maintenance (O&M) of wastewater system ■ Provide stand-by generators for uninterrupted power ■ Train operators	■ Standby generators ■ Emergency response system ■ O&M schedules ■ Regularity of training	■ Document checking ■ Periodic audit ■ No of incidents and complaints	Monthly	KUKL/ KVWSMB
Sewer cleaning	Risk of communicable diseases	■ Provide trainings to workers on Occupational Health and Safety (OHS)	■ Number of trainings conducted	■ Quiz and interviews ■ Audit of OHS policy ■ Number of workers trained	Monthly	KUKL/ KVWSMB

ANNEX I (D): OUTLINE OF A BIDDING DOCUMENT

MELAMCHI WATER SUPPLY PROJECT

Melamchi Diversion Scheme
CONTRACT NO. MDS/DT/01:
Headworks and Diversion Tunnel Construction
Bid Documents

Table of Contents

ANNEX I (E): OUTLINE OF A SITE-SPECIFIC ENVIRONMENTAL MANAGEMENT PLAN

1. Project Description
   1.1 Introduction
   1.2 Activities to be carried out (title, type, scale, and material requirement, trench excavation, laying and backfilling, reinforcement and concreting of the reservoirs or digester tanks)
   1.3 Project Detail (components, with details as described in the bill of quantity and drawing, linear projects sections when the pipe size changes, manholes details, sensitive receivers details, for point projects details of the components location)
   1.4 Location and base map of the project area divided into sections based on specific environmental attributes (alignment passing though core settlement, heritage/temple/religious areas, sensitive receptors such as hospital and schools/college, open field, drainage crossings, landslide areas, major trunk road, narrow lanes, major road crossing, river or drainage crossing etc.) and other point locations with specific functions such as treatment plant, labor camp, engineer's site office, quarry site, batching plant site, spoil disposal site etc.)

2. Safeguard Mechanism Established. Explain how safeguard mechanism will function; who will be the responsible persons such as authorized safeguard staff and safety staff with qualification; line of communication and coordination mechanism with the Project Implementation Directorate (PID), design and supervision consultant (DSC), and community awareness and safeguards support consultant (CASSC); and environmental management plan (EMP) assurance monitoring, documentation, and reporting. Present organogram with name of responsible staff and contact address.

3. Site-specific Environmental Description. For each section or location of the proposed structure provide description of physical, biological, and socio-economic & cultural environment. Mention the global positioning system (GPS) coordinates of key areas and supplement by photo and maps.

4. Activity, Potential Impact and Mitigation Measure. It will have two sections. The first will be generic and common to all issues, which will be described by following EMP attached to bidding document or contract. Second section will be identification of particular area of impact due to implementation of the work based on the baseline condition of that particular site such as steep slope, river bank erosion, wetland, gully, vegetation, sensitive receptors, core settlement, narrow lane, agriculture field, solid waste deposit, flora and fauna, ancient archaeological monument, old and dilapidated houses at risk due to any vibration during construction, and so on.
   The area of impact to be discussed for generic conditions could be following:

   4.1 Topography
   4.2 Soil condition
   4.3 Spoil management
   4.4 Topsoil stockpile and reuse
   4.5 Natural drainage
   4.6 Sedimentation and erosion control
   4.7 Construction material transportation and storage
   4.8 Quarry and borrow areas
   4.9 Drainage crossing
   4.10 Air quality, water quality, noise level, and vibration

4.11   Vegetation removal

4.12   Workers camp and facilities

4.13   Camp wastewater management

4.14   Camp solid waste management

4.15   Transportation, loading, unloading of pipes

4.16   Health and safety of workers, medical facility with health worker, and emergency arrangements

4.17   Slipping and tripping hazards

4.18   Proper techniques for trenching and shoring

4.19   Sludge management

4.20   Odor nuisance to the proximity of treatment plants

4.21   Traffic control when working on mains adjacent to roadways

4.22   Accidental fall in work trench

4.23   Accident and emergency protocol

4.24   Gas detection and rescue tripod and other equipment ready while working in confined spaces

4.25   Fall protection measures while working at height

4.26   Heritage Impact Assessment with mitigation measures

4.27   Environmental and safety awareness and training to workers

4.28   Reinstatement of community/public services and facilities

4.29   Community consultation and safety

The area of impact to be discussed for generic and site-specific conditions could be following:

5.   Activity, Potential Impact and Mitigation Measure (site-specific impacts). A section on site-specific mitigation measure and monitoring plan in the sections/plots along with details on action, impact, mitigation measure specific to the site, method, schedule, responsibility and cost (could be presented in a tabular matrix). The details may entail all or some of the issues discussed in section 4 above.

6.   Environmental Management and Monitoring Plan

6.1   Impact, mitigation measure, and implementation plan

6.2   Detail of air, water, and noise monitoring plan

6.3   Occupational health and safety plan

6.4   Camp management plan

6.5   Emergency protocol

6.6   Traffic management

6.7   Workers code of conduct

6.8   Accident report format

7.   Equipment, resources, and funds

8.   Contact details of the contractor's authorized staff designated for safeguard and safety assurance and reporting on site-specific environmental management plan compliance and coordinate on corrective measures as instructed by the employer's staff (PID/DSC/CASSC)

9.   Annexes

- Checklist for housekeeping
- Checklist for staging, scaffolding, and formwork
- Checklist for plant and equipment
- Checklist for material storage
- Checklist for excavation and backfilling in trenches
- Checklist and procedural manual for heritage-related impacts

ANNEX I (F): STRUCTURE OF A MONITORING REPORT

Environmental Compliance Monitoring Report
ADB Loan-..........................: Semiannual Environmental Compliance Monitoring Report
(Date.............................)

ABBREVIATIONS

ADB	–	Asian Development Bank
BDS	–	Bulk Distribution System
CASSC	–	Community Awareness and Safeguard Support Consultant
DMA	–	District Metering System
DNI	–	Distribution Network Improvement
DPD	–	Deputy Project Director
DSC	–	Design and Supervision Consultants
EIA	–	Environment Impact Assessment
EMP	–	Environmental Management Plan
GON	–	Government of Nepal
GRC	–	Grievance Redress Committee
GRM	–	Grievance Redress Mechanism
IEE	–	Initial Environmental Examination
KUKL	–	Kathmandu Upatyaka Khanepani Limited
KVWSIP	–	Kathmandu Valley Water Supply Improvement Project
MOPE	–	Ministry of Population and Environment
MoWS	–	Ministry of Water Supply
MLD	–	Millions of Liters per Day
NAAQS	–	National Ambient Air Quality Standards
OHS	–	Occupational Health and Safety
PD	–	Project Director
PID	–	Project Implementation Directorate
PM	–	Project Manager
PPE	–	Personnel Protective Equipment
TOR	–	Terms of Reference
WTP	–	Water Treatment Plant

TABLE OF CONTENTS

4. **Environmental Monitoring and Compliance with the Environmental Management Plan**
    4.1 Compliance with Contractor's Site-Specific Environmental Management Plan (discuss each issue with fact and figure)
    4.2 Compliance with Contractor's Occupational Health and Safety Plan (discuss each issue with fact and figure)
    4.3 Compliance with Emergency Protocol and Standard Operating Procedure for COVID-19 (discuss each issue with fact and figure)

5. **Compliance Status with Loan Covenants on Environment (short description on compliance and mention that detail is in the Annex)**

6. **Status of Safeguards Compliance to Issues Recorded in the last Environmental Monitoring Report and Action Plans Agreed in the Aide Memoire of Last Project Review Mission of ADB**

7. **Communication and Stakeholder Consultation**

8. **Capacity Building and Training**

9. **Grievance Redress Mechanism**
    9.1. Grievance Redress Mechanism Established
    9.2 Complaints Received during the Reporting Period
    9.3 Overall Status of Resolution of Complaints

10. **Information Disclosure During Reporting Period**

11. **Summary of Key Issues and Corrective Actions**
    11.1. Key Issues
    11.2. Corrective Action Plan Agreed with Contractor

12. **Area of Focus for the Next Reporting Period**

13. **Conclusion and Recommendation**

LIST OF ANNEXES

ANNEX I (G): EXAMPLE OF AN APPROVAL LETTER (ROAD-CUT PERMIT)

नेपाल सरकार

भौतिक पूर्वाधार तथा यातायात मन्त्रालय

सडक विभाग

संघीय सडक सुपरिवेक्षण तथा अनुगमन कार्यालय, काठमाडौं

सडक डिभिजन काठमाडौं

मिनभवन, काठमाडौं

फोन नं.   : ४४६५४५७

फ्याक्स नं. : ४४६५४५७

email : droktm1@dor.gov.np

droktm1@gmail.com

पत्र सं. :

च.नं. : ०५४६१०६१६९

मिति : २०७९।०१।०८

श्री काठमाडौं उपत्यका खानेपानी लि.,

आयोजना कार्यान्वयन निर्देशनालय,

अनामनगर ।

विषय : सडक संरचना खन्न स्वीकृति दिइएको सम्बन्धमा ।

प्रस्तुत विषयमा त्यस कार्यालयको प.सं. ०७८।०७९ च.नं. ९०६ मिति २०७८।१२।२१ को पत्रबाट HDD प्रविधिबाट पाइपलाइन विछ्याउने कार्यका लागि खनिएको सडक संरचना त्यस कार्यालयबाटै यथास्थितिमा पुनस्थापना गर्ने गरी सडक खन्न स्वीकृति माग भएकोमा श्री सडक विभाग, संघीय सडक सुपरीवेक्षण तथा अनुगमन कार्यालय, काठमाडौं र त्यस कार्यालय विच मिति २०७८।१०।२३ मा भएको समझदारी पत्र (MOU) का शर्तहरू अनिवार्य रुपमा कार्यान्वयन हुने गरी तथा पैदलयात्री, यातायात आवागमनमा बाधा नपर्ने गरी, पाइपलाइन विछ्याउने कार्य पश्चात् तत्काल सडक संरचनाको सतह मिलाउने एवं सडक संरचना मर्मत नभएसम्म दुर्घटना हुन नदिन सुरक्षाका उचित उपायहरू अवलम्बन गर्ने तथा दुर्घटना भएमा सोको जवाफदेही सडक संरचना खन्ने कार्यालय नै हुने शर्तमा उल्लेखित पत्रसाथ प्राप्त Revised work schedule अनुसार माग भए वमोजिम सामाखुसी रानीवारी सांग्रिला होटल सडक खण्ड (१३०० मिटर) र गोगंबु चोक रेडन कलेज गल्कोपाखा सडक खण्ड (१८५६ मिटर) मा प्रत्येक ५०-१०० मिटरमा नदोहोरिने गरी २ मि. x २.५ मि. सडक यस डिभिजनका प्राविधिकहरूसंग प्रत्यक्ष समन्वय गरी HDD प्रविधिबाट पाइपलाइन विछ्याउने कार्यका लागि सडक संरचना खन्न स्वीकृति दिइएको व्यहोरा अनुरोध छ ।

बोधार्थ :

- श्री संघीय सडक सुपरीवेक्षण तथा अनुगमन कार्यालय, काठमाडौं ।
- श्री महानगरीय ट्राफिक प्रहरी महाशाखा, रामशाहपथ ।
- श्री काठमाडौं उपत्यका खानेपानी लिमिटेड, केन्द्रीय कार्यालय, त्रिपुरेश्वर ।
- ई. श्री हरि कुमार ठकुरी, सडक डिभिजन काठमाडौं:

आवश्यक समन्वय तथा MOU अनुसारको कार्यको सुपरीवेक्षण गर्नु हुन ।

(ई. नारायण प्रसाद निहुरे)

डिभिजन प्रमुख

ANNEX I (H): EXAMPLES OF NOTICE TO CORRECT LETTER TO CONTRACTOR FOR NONCOMPLIANCE

Sample 1.

Letter No.:   Date:

To

....

....

Dear Sir / Madam,

Subject: Contract Package ....

        Notice to Correct: Instruction to comply with required mitigation measure at ....

In reference to the above subject, it was observed that manhole cleaning works in the middle of the road under contract no ...... of ...... project at .... was being carried out without complying with the required safety preparatory measures (joint monitoring checklist and reference photo is attached with this letter). Full compliance with the required safety measures cannot be compromised and is a must while working in such a risky situation at the middle of the road having high traffic movements. In this regard, we hereby instruct the contractor to urgently undertake the following corrective safety measure to continue work in that area and inform us of the compliance by ....date........

1. Place hard barricade around the working area and shoring in the trench or pit
2. Place informatory signboard and red flag at required locations to alert the speeding traffic of the ongoing work
3. All the workers and staff use full set of PPE before entering the work area
4. All measures to work inside confined space shall be followed before starting work (e.g., inside pipe)

We inform you that we will be compelled to take the action as stipulated in contract clause ....in case the state of non-compliance continues beyond the agreed deadline.

Regards

_____

Team Leader
DSC ....

Attached:
1. Joint monitoring checklist
2. Photograph

CC:

Sample 2.

Letter No.:   Date:

To

....

....

Dear Sir / Madam,

Subject: Contract Package ....
           Urgent Need to Improve the Safety Condition at Workplace particularly related with work in Confined Space

The copy of the Minutes of the Meeting held on .... jointly agreeing to urgently improve the safety arrangements made and protocols followed at the workplace particularly while "working in a confined space" is attached for your reference and immediate compliance. Attached with the letter are the following copies for your ready reference:

- Minutes of Meeting
- Safety Protocols while working in a Confined Space
- OHS Audit Report with recommendation
- Concerned section of the OHS Plan

Please note that maintaining safety is one of the highest priorities of the employer, which will not be compromised. Hence, we anticipate the contractor will take immediate action to correct the shortcomings as suggested in the OHS Audit Report and as agreed during the meeting to comply with the recommendations of the report and contractor's own OHS Plan within the agreed deadline as recorded in the minutes. If the contractor does not respond as agreed and the state of non-compliance is found to continue beyond the agreed date, the engineer will be compelled to suspend the work as per the clause 8.8 and take further action as per the clause ..... of the contract.

Looking forward for quick compliance as agreed, we remain

Sincerely yours

_____

Team Leader
DSC ....

Attached:
1. Joint monitoring checklist
2. Photograph

CC:

ANNEX I (I): EXAMPLE OF A LETTER FOR WORKSHOP (TRANNING TO WORKERS BEFORE COMMISSIONING)

Letter No.:   Date:

To

....

....

Dear Sir / Madam,

Subject: Contract Package ....

           Preparations to ensure safeguard compliance and worker and community safety during the commissioning of the system

 We discussed in the workshop of ....that intensive commissioning activities will commence in the next three months. Hence, it was agreed that the contractor will start all the required preparations in order to ensure no untoward safeguard and safety incident occurs during the process. Preparations will also be made to take immediate remedial action to handle any situation that may occur during the commissioning by ensuring safeguard and safety protocol.

We have attached following with this letter for your ready reference and action:

- Minutes agreed during the .... workshop
- Workshop presentation detail
- Tentative schedule and location of testing & commissioning

Full time presence of safeguard and safety staff shall be ensured while implementing the work.

Yours sincerely,

————————————————

Team Leader
DSC

Attached:

1. Minutes agreed during the workshop

2. Workshop presentation detail

3. Tentative schedule and location of testing & commissioning

4. Safety protocol

CC:

ANNEX I (J): A SAMPLE LETTER FOR APPROVAL OF TREE CUTTING

Letter No.:   Date:

To

....

....

Dear Sir / Madam,

Subject: Contract Package ....

                Approval for tree cutting at ....

This is in response to your letter Ref: VA-CRP-DSC6-L-2081 dated 23 December 2019 with a request for approval to clear tree no. 68 and 69 in the site .... at .... We hereby confirm our clearance to clear the said trees at a condition to adhere and fully comply with the Clause 47 on Environmental Management Plan (EMP): Vegetation Clearance in the Special Condition of Contract. Please maintain close coordination with required stakeholders and the Environment Expert of DSC.... while clearing the trees. Please ensure taking all safety measures while cutting the tree and stockpile the logs at the location approved by the engineer by ensuring no tree parts will be used by the contractor or workers for burning, cooking and heating purpose; or using in construction work without approval from engineer.

Yours sincerely,

_____

Team Leader
DSC

Attachment:
CC:

ANNEX I (K): SAMPLE LETTER FOR COMPENSATORY TREE PLANTATION

Letter No.:   Date:

To

....

....

Dear Sir / Madam,

Subject: Contract Package ....
            Approval for compensatory plantation and greening of the site

In reference to above subject, you were permitted to cut .... number of trees in the .... site. However, please note that such permission does not relieve the Contractor from any of its obligations, duties and responsibilities under the contract towards safeguard and safety compliances. Hence, you are instructed to comply the mitigation measure in accordance with the Environment Management Plan under the Table 1 in Vegetation Clearance suggested in Clause 47 of the Special Condition of Contract. According to the requirements for mitigation measure, "the tree saplings should be planted and reared at the rate of 25 saplings for each felled tree". In this regard, a total of 2,525 tree saplings should be planted and reared as a compensatory measure for the felled trees.

Handling plantation is associated with its rate of survival. Hence, you are free to choose establishing nursery at the site or procure saplings from government or private nursery. The type of trees shall be selected in consultation with the Environment Consultant of DSC, which shall encompass the perennial, seasonal, decorative, flowering plants and proposed location for their plantation presented on a site map. You may also choose to either do the plantation and rearing yourself or hire a nursery to plant tress, grass and shrubs and develop garden with proper landscaping in the area. We request you to submit your tree plantation and vegetation plan for the site by ...date...... by addressing the issues discussed above.

Yours sincerely

_____

Team Leader
DSC

Attachment:
1. Clause 47 of the Special Condition of Contract
CC:

ANNEX I (L): SAMPLE LETTER TO CONTRACTOR FOR APPOINTMENT OF SAFEGUARD/SAFETY OFFICER

Letter No.:   Date:

To

....

....

Dear Sir / Madam,

Subject: Contract Package ....
           Approval of Environmental Safeguard Officer and Safety Officer

We received the curriculum vitae of the environmental safeguard officer, and safety officer proposed to be mobilized in the project under the contract by the contractor.

We reviewed the curriculum vitae and supporting certificates of the proposed candidates, and found them to be qualified for the position. Hence, we have no objection to appoint Mr/Ms ....as environmental safeguard officer and Mr/Ms ....as a safety officer. Please note that both the officers should be exclusively dedicated to monitor and manage their subject-matter area and should be mobilized full-time before field mobilization. Any replacement of staff in future should be equivalent to the original candidates and duly approved by the employer. Please also note that work shall not be allowed to be implemented in the absence of these two full-time experts in the project.

Yours sincerely,

_____

Team Leader
DSC

Attachment:
CC:

ANNEX I (M): SAMPLE LETTER FOR SUBMISSION OF INITIAL ENVIRONMENTAL EXAMINATION TERMS OF REFERENCE FOR APPROVAL

Letter No.:   Date:

To,

Subject: Submission of Terms of Reference (TOR) of the Distribution Network Improvement (DNI) 9 A-1

Dear Sir / Madam,

We would like to submit the attached Terms of Reference (TOR) for conducting IEE of Contract Package DNI 9A-1 for your review and approval. We look forward to soon receive your response in order to expedite the work.

Thank you for your kind consideration.

Yours sincerely,

....
Team Leader, DSC

CC
1.
Attached:

1. Terms of Reference for IEE

ANNEX I (N): SAMPLE LETTER FOR COMPENSATION TO THE INJURED WORKER

Letter No.:   Date:

To,

....

....

Subject: Compensation to the injured worker

Dear Sir / Madam,

In reference to the above subject, your report has been reviewed. It is reported that all the medical expenses are covered and wages for the period of treatment is paid by the contractor.

As per Sub clause no 22.2.3 of Clause 22 of General Conditions of Contract (Volume I of contract document), "The contractor shall comply with all relevant Labor Laws applicable to the Contractor's Personnel". And as per Labor Regulation 2075 (Chapter 8 rule 49), "In case a worker or employee, after being injured in course of doing the works designated by the Enterprise, is unable to work and is required to undergo treatment staying at home or Hospital, the Proprietor shall have to provide the full remuneration in case of treatment in the Hospital; half of the remuneration in case of treatment undergone at home for that period". Hence, we anticipate contractor has paid all the eligible amount to the worker.

Yours sincerely,

_____

Team Leader

Att:

CC: PID:

   PID:

ANNEX I (O): SAMPLE OF STANDARD SIGNBOARDS DESIGNED BY THE PROJECT IMPLEMENTATION DIRECTORATE

A. Traffic Diversion Board

Board Details:

- Should be kept in 0.61-meter iron stand
- Breadth of board: 0.6 meter
- Length of board: 0.9 meter
- 60% of the board area should be covered by diversion sign
- Letter size: Font size should be as given in the board: clearly visible from at least 50-meter distance
- Place the board at the location of diversion

B. Work-in-Progress (Road Closure) Signage Board

Board Details

- Length of board: 0.9 meter
- Breadth of board: 0.9 meter
- Should be kept in 0.61-meter iron stand
- Letter size: Font size should be as given in the board: clearly visible from at least 50-meter distance
- Place the board at the entry points of lane

C. No Entry Signage Board

Board Details

- Length of board: 0.6 meter
- Breadth of board: 1.2 meters
- Should be kept in 0.61-meter iron stand
- 60% of the board area should be covered by no entry logo at the center
- Location at all sites where unauthorized entry is not permitted (camp, worksite, material stockpile area, etc.)

D. Personal Protective Equipment Use Signage Board

Board Details

- Breadth of board: 1 meter
- Length of board: 1 meter
- Should be kept in 0.61 meter iron stand
- Location at worksite, workshops, entrance to camp, etc.

E. Danger Signage Tape or Board

सावधान ! सावधान ! सावधान ! सावधान ! सावधान ! साव

काठमाण्डौ उपत्यका खानेपानी तथा सरसफाइ आयोजना /आयोजना कार्यान्वयन निर्देशनालय ! काठमाण्डौ उपत्यका खानेपानी तथा सरसफाइ आयोजना /आयोजना कार्यान्वयन निर्देशनालय

Breadth of board: 0.076 meter (7.6 centimeters)

F. Project Information Board (Site Specific)

काठमाण्डौ उपत्यका खानेपानी तथा सरसफाइ आयोजना

आयोजना कार्यान्वयन निर्देशनालय

मेलम्ची खानेपानी उप–आयोजना– २

काठमाण्डौ उपत्यका खानेपानी लिमिटेड

अनामनगर, काठमाण्डौ

४२८६९९६ ४२५८७७

डि.एन.आइ नं			
पाइप किसिम		पाइप साइज	
शुरु मिति		अन्त्य मिति	
निर्माण व्यवसायी			

Board Details

- Length of board: 2 meters
- Breadth of board: 1.5 meters
- Should be kept in 0.61 meter stand

G. COVID-19 Prevention Informative Board

Should be kept at entrance, camp, work area, medical facility, dining area, etc.

ANNEX I (P): SAMPLE OF SAFEGUARD PROVISIONS IN BIDDING DOCUMENT (Sample from SN-03 Package, PID. Bid type: Single Stage Two Envelop Procedure)

A. Safeguard Items in the Bill of Quantity of Bidding Document

Part No. A: General Items, Daywork and Provisional Sum
Work No. A1 : General Items

Item No.	Description of Works	Unit	Quantity	Rate (NRs.) (in figure)	Rate (NRs.) (In words)	Amount (NRs.)
A	**GENERAL OBLIGATIONS**					
A.1	Providing and installation of project sign boards with size of 1.8m x1.2 m and demolishing after completion of work of as per specification (Spec. 2.3.1)	Nos.	4			

Part No. A: General Items, Daywork and Provisional Sum
Work No. A1 : General Items

Item No.	Description of Works	Unit	Quantity	Rate (NRs.) (in figure)	Rate (NRs.) (In words)	Amount (NRs.)
C.3	Placement of dedicated 1 no Archeologist officer for 6 months period (Spec 2.4).	Months	6			
C.4	Provide temporary hoardings and barricades for protection of work area with flashing lights during excavation in the construction site as per drawing, specification and instruction (Spec 2.6.3, see drawing in Vol. II Annex II)	Nos.	60			

Part No. A: General Items, Daywork and Provisional Sum
Work No. A1 : General Items

Item No.	Description of Works	Unit	Quantity	Rate (NRs.) (in figure)	Rate (NRs.) (In words)	Amount (NRs.)
C	**Environmental Management Plan (EMP) Implementation and Safeguards**					
C.1	Providing and installing safety signage boards, caution tapes and green nets, water sprinkling three times a day during construction works, monitoring the sound and vibrations of machine and tools, regular health check-ups in three equal time interval, trainings and awareness programs to contractor's labors, personal protective equipment, first aid kits, fire extinguishers, traffic control devices etc during construction works as per specification and engineer's instruction. (Spec. 2.1.6). Also refer to EMP and PID Safeguard Manual.	Months	18			
C.2	Placement of dedicated 2 nos. Safety officers throughout contract period for maintaining safety and protection against accidents including traffic control and EMP safeguard compliances with one standby emergency vehicle. Also refer to EMP and PID Safeguard Manual (Spec. 2.4)	Months	18*2			

Part No. A: General Items, Daywork and Provisional Sum

Work No. A1 : General Items

Item No.	Description of Works	Unit	Quantity	Rate (NRs.) (in figure)	Rate (NRs.) (In words)	Amount (NRs.)
E	Providing and installation of Temporary Walkway of steel chequered sheet (Spec. 2.1.6.3)	Sq m	600			
	Grand Total Amount of WORK A1 of Part A =					

Part No. A: General Items, Daywork and Provisional Sum

Work No. A3 : Provisional Sum

Item No.	Description of Works	Unit	Quantity	Rate (NRs.) (in figure)	Rate (NRs.) (in words)	Amount (NRs.)
A	**Provisional Sum for additional Environmental Mitigation Measures, Social Safeguards and items not covered (Spec 2.7).**					
A.1	Provision for mitigation measures of unanticipated environmental/cultural heritage impacts and social safeguard, Reinstating or relocating public utilities within land services, ie. Electric pole, transformer, street lightning, other electric line accessories, telephone poles, other telecom network infrastructures, unanticipated water supply pipe lines, water supply fittings and accessories, etc; reinstatement of affected pavement not specified in Work No. C1; removal of archaeological chance findings and handling to a designated location in or near Patan Durbar Square; reinstatement of damaged structures during construction activities, allowance for supervision for DOA personnel and items not covered in the BOQ etc. including supply of necessary materials, labors, equipment, tools and installation all complete work as per specification and instructed by the Engineer.	PS	1	29,600,000.00	Twenty-Nine million six hundred thousand only	29,600,000.00

Part No. B: Civil Works

Work No. B1: Surface Dressing, Earthwork, Sand Filling and Other Earth Material Related Works

Item No.	Description of Works	Unit	Quantity	Rate (NRs.) (in figure)	Rate (NRs.) (In words)	Amount (NRs.)
14	Disposal of surplus excavated earthwork materials from construction site to disposing site (within 10km premises) including loading, unloading etc. all complete. (Spec No. 11.5.10)	Cu m	6446.34			
	Grand Total Amount of WORK B1 of Part B =					

B. Safeguard related provision in Volume II: Requirements

Personnel Requirements

1	Environment, Health and Safety Officer 1 nos.	BE or BSc in Environmental Engineering or Environmental science. Health and Safety Staff shall be accredited by an OHS institution	4 years' experience	2

2 ITEM OF GENERAL APPLICATION

2.1 EMPLOYER'S REQUIREMENT

The Employer's requirement given in this section shall be read in conjunction with Technical Specification and Conditions of Contract.

2.1.6 Site Safety and Utilities

2.1.6.1. Site Safety

In order to improve the general vehicular traffic condition and to guarantee public safety from and around the work the contractor shall provide all labor and material, and construct and maintain temporary traffic diversion throughout the construction activities, to the directive and approval of the Engineer. It is therefore recognized that there is a particular responsibility placed upon the contractor to take special precautions for public safety and to minimize the scale and extent of disruption to pubic and commercial life. Plan for traffic diversion shall always be submitted to the Engineer and to the traffic police for their prior approval.

The contractor shall ensure that the work are carried out in a safe manner, according to internationally accepted guidelines on safe working procedure and to the satisfaction of the Engineer. The contractor shall strictly follow IFC EHS guideline 2007 to safeguard environmental health and safety at construction sites and other construction related facilities.

The following requirements shall be complied by the Contractor:

a) Excavation – The trenches have to be excavated in a single step as the width available will not permit stepping of trench. The contractor should mobilize excavation machinery suitable for excavating deep trenches, at the same time ensuring that the machinery provided are less than 2.4m wide and can work from the road while lowering the pipes into deep trench.

b) All excavations shall be adequately supported to avoid collapses. Effective safety barriers shall be erected with warning signs and covered by green net around all open excavations to the satisfaction of the Engineer (See Vol II Annex 2 and Annex 3).

Struts shall not be used as ladders. For the purpose of access to the base of trench the contractor shall provide proper and suitably secured ladder.

Reflective vests wearing shall be worn by all workmen and, where necessary, temporary road signs and cone shall be provided to ensure a safe working area. While excavating along the road reserve, sufficiently strong and wide timber bridge shall be provided for pedestrian crossing.

As far a possible the excavation in front of entrances shall be backfilled the same day. Sufficient written notice (at least 3 days in advance) shall be given to the resident who may be affected by the excavation.

c) Personal Protective Equipment (PPE) and Protective Clothing- The contractor shall ensure that all personnel on site are supplied with necessary protective equipment and clothing such as protective aprons, safety helmets, goggles, face masks, ear muffs, gloves, boots, knee pads depending on the operation to be performed.

d) Scaffolding – Suitable and sufficient scaffolds shall be provided and properly maintained for all work that cannot safely be carried out from the ground or from part of the structure or from a ladder.

   Every scaffold shall be of suitable and sound material and of adequate strength for the purpose which it is used. Unless designed as an independent structure, every scaffold shall be rigidly connected to a part of the structure which is of sufficient strength to afford safe support. Protective headgear shall always be worn.

e) Lifting Devices – Every rope, chain pulley, bloc, hook, winch, crane, or other lighting gear used for raising or lowering pipes of as a means of suspending them shall be of good construction, sound material, adequate strength and free from defects. They shall be properly maintained and tested at regular intervals by a competent person, who shall be approved by the Engineer.

f) Working in existing manholes etc.- Checks shall be carried out before entry to ensure that the atmosphere is fit for respiration and no smoke, naked lights or flames are to be permitted in any sewer, manholes or chambers or in their vicinity.

g) The equipment which shall be made available shall include but not limited to following:

   - Lifting harness with ropes
   - Hand- lamps with spare batteries
   - First aid kit (including moist wipes, disposable gloves, sterile dressing , sterile eye pads, bandage, safety pins, distilled water, scissors etc.).
   - Protective gloves.
   - Rubber gloves
   - Breathing apparatus

h) Throughout the period of the contract, the contractor shall provide safety helmets and reflective jackets to all Consultant's staff and visitors. Barriers must be provided to all excavations for the safety of the public and flagmen must be used for all items of plant for the safety of operatives, supervision staff and public.

i) The contractor shall at all times in the conduct of his work and that of his subcontractors adhere to the established rules and regulations concerning all safety matters at site such as the recommendation constrained in the 'Manual of Accident Preventive in Construction", published by the Association of General Contractor of America, Inc., or other internationally recognized recommendation to the extent that such provision do not conflict with the applicable laws. This is especially important wherever it is necessary to enable the free passage of the public through the site.

j) The contractor's safety officer shall have the qualification and the authority to issue instructions to the contractor's personnel regarding protection measures to prevent accident.

k) During construction the safety officer shall have the qualification and the authority to issue instruction to the contractor's personnel regarding protection measures to prevent accidents.

   If and where required, the Contractor shall erect and maintain suitable and approved temporary fencing to enclose such areas of the works and areas of land occupied by the Contractor within the site as may be necessary to implement his obligation under the Condition of Contract. Where temporary fencing has to be erected alongside a public road, foot-path etc., it shall be of the type required by and shall be erected to the satisfaction of the authority concerned.

l) All open excavations along pipelines shall be protected sufficiently to keep out livestock and ensure the safety of workmen and public.

m) Where work is to be carried out in the proximity of buildings, bridges, tank or other structures, the Contractor shall take all necessary precautions, including shoring and strutting, where necessary, to ensure the safety of the structures that are at risk.

n) The contractor shall be responsible for all damages or injury, which may be caused on any property by trespassing by the contractor's or his subcontractor's employee. In the course of their employment, whether the said trespass was committed with or without the consent or knowledge of the contractor.

Measurement and Payment: Implementing EMP and Social Safeguards will be considered as one job and payment will be made on the monthly basis for establishment and implementing at least all the following mitigations for the possible environmental impacts and in order to maintain safety during the time of construction.

i. Contractor will be responsible to provide temporary hoardings/hard barricade during trench excavation in the construction site to prevent unauthorized entry and to maintain safety.

ii. Safety signboards, caution tapes and green nets shall also be provided as and when required during construction activities.

iii. Contractor will sprinkle water three times a day during construction to prevent dust generation.

iv. Contractor will further monitor the sound and vibration of machine, tools, etc. during construction work by using in site hiring instruments at its own cost and submit reports to the Engineer. This is to avoid damage to vulnerable and old structures. Sound and Vibration shall be within acceptable limit as specified in the standards or as directed by the Engineer.

v. Contractor will further supply potable water to affected community due to construction activity.

vi. Regular health check-ups of labors during the contract period shall be conducted by the contractor.

vii. All labors will be equipped by personal protective equipment (PPE) and clothing and workers will be required to use applicable PPE during construction depending on their tasks.

viii. Contractor will make available first aid kits, fire extinguisher, and an emergency vehicle close to the construction site all the time during construction.

2.1.6.2 Contractor's plant to reduce noise level

When working in built-up areas, the contractor shall use suitable and effective noise silencing devices for pneumatic tools and other plant that would otherwise cause a noise level exceeding 85 dB during excavation and other work. Alternatively, they shall, by means of barrier, effectively isolate the source of any such noise in order to comply with above requirement.

2.1.6.3 Detours and Traffic Management

The contractor shall program his work in such a way that, wherever the temporary closure of street sections to public thoroughfare cannot be avoided, the duration of traffic diversion can be kept as short as possible. No streets shall be closed, and no detours shall be introduced, and no traffic diverted until the contractor's proposals have been approved by the Engineer and the appropriate Government authorities, such as the Roads Department and police.

Where work is to be carried out on public roads, the Contractor shall give notice to the Engineer sufficiently in advance of the date (at least ... working days before) on which he wishes to commence such work.

The Contractor shall be responsible for obtaining the permission of the Employer, Road Department and the police for works he intends to carry out in public roads. Two copies of the contractor's proposal to the relevant authorities shall be submitted to the Engineer. One copy of all obtained approval shall be submitted to the engineer. The Contractor attention is drawn on the fact that processing of the documentation required by the local authorities prior to the cutting of existing public roads take approximately 30 days. During the Monsoon period (June to August) no road cutting is normally allowed. Kathmandu Valley holds many local festivals. So planning for the excavation in various stretches has to be done in advance keeping in view these festival dates.

Detours shall be selected in such a way that the inconvenience to the affected traffic as well as to the inhabitants of the affected areas is kept to a minimum. The contractor shall supply and place the standard traffic control device for the diversion of traffic.

Walkaways and sidewalk shall be provided with chequered plates or planks. They shall be kept clear of excavated materials or other obstruction and no sidewalk shall be undermined unless shores are provided or protected by suitable means to carry a minimum live load of 10kN/m^2. If planks are used for raised walkways, runways, or sidewalks, they shall be laid parallel to the length of the walk and fastened together against displacement. Planks shall be uniform in thickness and all exposed ends shall be provided with beveled cleats to prevent tripping.

The Contractor shall furnish, install, and maintain at all times during the execution of the works all necessary traffic signs, barricades, lights, signals and other traffic control devices, including flagging.

2.1.6.4 Preparation of a Traffic Management Plan

The contractor shall prepare a Traffic Management Plan (TMP) that shall be approved by the Engineer.

2.1.6.7 Construction Barricade

The contractor shall furnish hard barricades of the specified type (drawing for reference in Annex 2) required in the project to confirm to the requirement stated in the item "Site Safety" and as directed by the Engineer. The Contractor shall furnish a sufficient number of construction barricades required for the traffic patterns and people's mobility for all operations which are being undertaken concurrently. The barricades shall be constructed in a neat and skilled workmanship to the satisfaction of the Engineer.

2.1.11.1 Material Storage

The contractor shall not keep the construction material on the road. For this purpose, the contractor should arrange the material stockyard near the construction site and the material should be transported to the work site only when necessary. The stock yard should be installed in a safe, dry area and a protective wall must be installed and material covered to prevent the loss of material by rainfall. In particular, cements should be stored in proper enclosed storage areas.

2.1.11.4 Sanitation & Toilet

The Contractor shall provide throughout the period of construction and shall maintain and clean, suitable, gender sensitive and sufficient number of toilet for use by their employees. They shall ensure that their employees do not foul the site but make proper use of the toilet.

2.1.11.5 Disposal of Sewage and Waste

The Contractor shall make provision for the discharge or disposal from the camp, offices and the works of all water as well as all liquid and solid waste products generated. The methods of disposal shall be to the satisfaction of the Engineer.

2.1.11.6 Medical Arrangement

The Contractor shall make arrangements for treatment of injuries and sick person in first-aid units or in such other wards.

Notwithstanding the minimum requirement prescribed above, the Contractor shall be responsible for the adequacy of all the arrangements made as per the provision of the contracts.

2.3 Other Requirements

2.3.1 Project Signboards

Project Signboards of 1.8 meter X 1.2 meter size shall be provided in the beginning and at the end of each active sites. These signboards shall be painted in approved color and provided with detail information as mentioned in Annex-2 of the Special provisions for Sewer Works. The contractor shall remove the sign board after completion of work.

2.3.3 Cutting of Trees

No trees shall be cut without the permission of the Engineer. If trees have to be cut, this shall form an extra item. For the purpose of the specification a tree shall be defined as that having 0.3 meter circumference of the trunk at 1 meter from the ground.

2.3.5 Leave Clean Work Site

On completion, all work site and camp areas shall be cleaned, rubbish removed and the site cleaned of surplus material, debris and other accumulations and everything left in clean and orderly condition by the contractor.

ANNEX I (Q): SAMPLE OF SAFEGUARD PROVISIONS IN THE CONTRACT AGREEMENT

A. Safeguard in the General Conditions of Contract

Major safeguard-related items in the general conditions of contract are given below.

4.8 Safety Procedures	The Contractor shall: (a) comply with all applicable safety regulations, (b) take care for the safety of all persons entitled to be on the Site, (c) use reasonable efforts to keep the Site and Works clear of unnecessary obstruction so as to avoid danger to these persons, (d) provide fencing, lighting, guarding and watching of the Works until completion and taking over under Clause 10 [*Employer's Taking Over*], and (e) provide any Temporary Works (including roadways, footways, guards and fences) which may be necessary, because of the execution of the Works, for the use and protection of the public and of owners and occupiers of adjacent land.
4.17 Contractor's Equipment	The Contractor shall be responsible for all Contractor's Equipment. When brought on to the Site, Contractor's Equipment shall be deemed to be exclusively intended for the execution of the Works. The Contractor shall not remove from the Site any major items of Contractor's Equipment without the consent of the Engineer. However, consent shall not be required for vehicles transporting Goods or Contractor's Personnel off Site.
6.7 Health and Safety	The Contractor shall at all times take all reasonable precautions to maintain the health and safety of the Contractor's Personnel. In collaboration with local health authorities, the Contractor shall ensure that medical staff, first aid facilities, sick bay and ambulance service are available at all times at the Site and at any accommodation for Contractor's and Employer's Personnel, and that suitable arrangements are made for all necessary welfare and hygiene requirements and for the prevention of epidemics. The Contractor shall appoint an accident prevention officer at the Site, responsible for maintaining safety and protection against accidents. This person shall be qualified for this responsibility, and shall have the authority to issue instructions and take protective measures to prevent accidents. Throughout the execution of the Works, the Contractor shall provide whatever is required by this person to exercise this responsibility and authority. The Contractor shall send, to the Engineer, details of any accident as soon as practicable after its occurrence. The Contractor shall maintain records and make reports concerning health, safety and welfare of persons, and damage to property, as the Engineer may reasonably require. HIV-AIDS Prevention. The Contractor shall conduct an HIV-AIDS awareness programme via an approved service provider, and shall undertake such other measures as are specified in this Contract to reduce the risk of the transfer of the HIV virus between and among the Contractor's Personnel and the local community, to promote early diagnosis and to assist affected individuals.

B. Safeguard in Particular Conditions of Contract

Major safeguard-related items are explained at Part B Specific Provision under the particular conditions of contract.

4.8	Safety Procedures	*Add the following subclause at the end of GCC Clause 4.8:* (a) The contractor shall adhere to international best practices on community and occupational health and safety such as the World Bank EHS guidelines on construction and decommissioning activities.[1] (b) The Contractor shall provide on his on cost all labour and materials and construct/install and maintain site safety, hard barricading, flexible green net, signboards, temporary day/light traffic diversions throughout the construction activities according to the specifications and provide Personal Protective Equipment (PPE) to all the labourers working at the construction site. (c) Contractor must take special precautions for public safety to minimise the scale and extent of disruption to public and commercial life. **1 % penalty will be deducted for non-compliance of occupational health and safety requirements as mentioned above under the respective IPC.**
4.18	Protection of the Environment	*Add the following sentence at the end of para 2. of GCC Sub-Clause 4.18:* The Contractor shall (a) comply with the measures relevant to the Contractor set forth in the Initial Environmental Examination (IEE), the Environmental Management Plan (EMP) (attached hereto as Appendix A), the site-specific EMP (SEMP) to be developed by the Contractor and approved by the PID and the Resettlement Plan (RP) (to the extent they concern impacts on affected people during construction); and any corrective or preventative actions set forth in a safeguards monitoring report; (b) allocate budget for implementing all activities and mitigation measures as indicated in the IEE, EMP, SEMP and social safeguard documents. ; (c) provide the Employer with a written notice of any unanticipated environmental, or resettlement risks or impacts that arise during construction, implementation or operation of the Works that were not considered in the IEE, the EMP, and the RP; (d) allocate an adequate Provisional Sum to cover the effective implementation and

monitoring of mitigation measures and/or activities not included in the BOQ, including mitigation measures for any unanticipated environmental impacts; (e) adequately record the condition of roads, structures, or other infrastructure prior to starting to transport materials and construction; (f) reinstate roads, pathways, and other local infrastructure to at least their pre-project condition upon the completion of construction; and (g) prepare SEMP based on IEE and EMPwith detailed provisions for local impacts associated with particular sites (including the World Heritage Site) and phases of construction before starting the construction works and obtaining SEMP approval at least one week before taking possession of any work site. No access to the site will be allowed until the SEMP is approved by the PID.

In addition, the Contractor shall have the following specific responsibilities:

(i) **Existing utilities**. The Contractor shall take special attention for management/taking care of the utilities with associated responsibilities as follows;
   a. Relocation of Utilities ;
   b. Repair of damaged water pipes of dia25mm and less - shall be undertaken before backfilling the excavated trench (i.e. within the same day of pipe laying if possible)
   c. Repair of damaged water and sewer pipes of dia 25mm and above - shall be undertaken within 2 days of the damage depending upon circumstances on his on cost;
   d. Repair of damage to all other utilities - on his on cost to the Contractor;
   e. Relocation and repair of damage to the utility is the responsibility of the Contractor. The Contractor shall need to coordinate the relocation and repair with the concerned Authority;
   f. The Employer/ Engineer can engage others at cost to undertake any non-compliance of the above said works;

(ii) **Trial trenches and trench stability**. The Contractor shall dig trial trenches as directed by the engineer at designated locations in order to exactly locate the underground utilities. The trial trenches shall be to the required size and full depth i.e. invert level of pipe. The work shall be carried out at Contractor's cost.For trenches deeper than 1.5 m or as directed by the Engineer, shoring is to be installed in order to stabilise the slope/cut.

(iii) **Spoils management.** The Contractor shall ensure that soil spoil and other construction debris that will not be used as fill will be cleared from the site regularly to avoid the proliferation of spoil stockpiles. Spoil will be disposedof at a site agreed with the PID. If the spoil is to be used as fill in other areas or construction projects, it will be subject to the PIU's approval. Care will be taken to ensure that spoil is kept free of general waste, sewage,hazardous wastes or any other contaminants that may render the material unsuitable as fill.All associated soil that will be used for backfilling at a later stage shall be removed offsite temporarily until it is needed. The following associated works shall also be undertaken:
   a. The backfill needs to be completed within the same day, immediately followed by reinstatement with sub base material within the same day and base material the following day unless due to unforeseen circumstances;
   b. The sub base and base material road surface shall be rolled

daily as required or minimum 4-5 days for removal of undulation after reinstatement;

c. Sealing of the pipe laid trench area with concrete asphalt shall be undertaken within one week of the pipe installation works of a particular stretch. No pipe laid trench area shall be left not sealed with concrete asphalt for more than 7 days;

d. Stone and brick pavements, particularly in heritage areas and old city areas shall be reinstated properly using required percentage of new stone and bricks within a day of opening the trench. Skilled labour in laying stone and brick pavements shall be kept at standby by the contractor at all times;

e. Contractor to have standby machinery (per say JCB and 10T roller) 24x7 to "rescue" any vehicles bogged in the trench area for a minimum 3-4 days after pipe laying for the particular day of road stretch that had been worked;

f. Contractor has to sprinkler water over pipe laid trench area using water trucks on a daily basis for a minimum 4-5 times a day or the number of times as instructed by the Engineer until the road is blacktopped; and

g. Contractor is reminded that the Employer/ Engineer can engage others at cost to undertake any non-compliance of the above said. Further, the Contractor agrees that a notice by way of a phone SMS to engage others shall be considered as contractually binding and that no other formal notices shall be required to be issued. Contractor shall be given the authorized numbers that will apply in the above case. (Any decision taken through SMS shall be recorded in written within 3 days);

(iv) **Dust.** The Contractor shall take all reasonable measures to minimize the generation of dust as a result of construction activities to the satisfaction of the Project Manager or equivalent officer. The Contractor's dust management planning should, as a minimum,include the following: (1) schedule of spraying water on unpaved areas and due attention to control of runoff; (2) Measures to ensure that material loads are properly covered during transportation; (3) Minimization of the areas disturbed at any one time and protection of exposed soil against wind erosion, e.g. by dampening with water or covering with straw or a tarp; (4) Location and treatment of material stockpiles taking into consideration prevailing wind directions and location of sensitive receptors; and (5) Reporting mechanism and action plan in case of excessive wind and dust conditions.

(v) **Noise.** Taking into consideration the urban context of the project the appropriate directional and intensity settings are to be maintained on all hooters and sirens, and the Contractor shall provide and use suitable and effective silencingdevices for tools, equipment and other construction utilities such that the noise level in inhabited areas and dwellings adjacent to the work areas will not exceed the applicable standards.

(vi) Where excess noise generation is unavoidable, the Contractor shall, by means of barriers, effectively isolate the source of any such noise in order to comply with the said regulations. The Contractor shall restrictany operations that may result in undue noise disturbance to those communities and dwellings neighboring the construction site to the hours of 07:00 to 21:00 Sunday to Friday. No work will be permitted on Saturdays unless otherwise agreed to with the Project Manager or equivalent officer. Neighboring businesses and places of residence that may be disrupted by such activity should be notified by the Contractor prior to commencement and provide an estimated schedule of the work.

(vii) **Vibration.** No equipment that will cause vibration shall be used during construction, particularly in areas of historical and/or archaeological significance. However, the Contractor should inspect nearby buildings to observe any structural instability or cracks, and inventory these with photographs.

(viii) **Vegetation.** Any removal of trees or vegetation should be reinstated to the same or better condition immediately after works are completed.

(ix) **Solid Waste and debris.** The Contractor will undertake a daily inspection of the construction site, ensuring that all litter and debris, whether his or not, is collected and disposed of responsibly. Stockpiling of spoil and construction materialsor debris will be done in a manner that minimizes its visual impact. Burning or open dumping of any waste is strictly prohibited.

(x) **Spills.** The contractor will develop a method statement for fuel storage, refueling and spills procedures. The method statement will outline:

   a. Fuel storage requirement (i.e. if fuel storage is required within the construction area, fuel containers will be stored within bounded areas with at least 110% volume of the amount of fuel stored or in portable bunds);

   b. Refueling procedures (e.g. refueling over drip trays);

   c. Spills procedures for containing and cleaning up oil/fuel spills (i.e. provision of spill kits incuding. absorbent materials etc.)

   d. Any soil contaminated (e.g. by oil) will be treated as hazardous waste and disposed of accordingly.

   e. The method statement will be reviewed, approved by the Project Manager or equivalent officer.

(xi) **Barricades.** The Contractor shall erect and maintain temporary barriers of the type and in the locations directed by the Project Manager or equivalent officer. Such barriers shall be erected before undertaking designated activities. Barriers are to be engineeredto withstand heavy winds and rains and must consider public safety (i.e. no sharp protrusions or edges, no tripping risks, major gaps and holes) and be sturdy enough for the intended purpose. Warning tape and netting alone are not deemed a sufficient barrierfor any active construction sites that involve machinery, open trenches and other hazards. Barriers should be inspected daily for health and safety risks and, where required, immediately repaired.

(xii) **Signage.** Advance road signage indicating the road detour and alternative routes. Provide sign boards for pedestrians to inform nature and duration of construction works, safety warnings, and contact numbers for concerns/complaints.

(xiii) **Daily Inspections.** Daily safety risk inspections of all pedestrian walkways and thoroughfares should be undertaken and where required immediate repairs and changes made.

(xiv) **Access to the Work Site.** The Contractor shall ensure that access to the site and associated infrastructure and equipment is off-limits to the public at all times during construction. As directed by the Project Manager or equivalent officer, the Contractor shall securethe site with barricades to ensure effective control of access to the site. The barricades shall be erected around the site and shall be maintained for the duration of each phase.

(xv) **Construction yard and site office.** The Contractor's camp should be surrounded by durable permanent fencing material to prevent unauthorized public access. The camp should be kept in a neat and orderly fashion, with proper disposal of solidwaste, vermin control, and access to potable water for all workers.

(xvi) **Workshop, equipment maintenance and storage.** All vehicles and equipment shall be kept in good working order. Leaking equipment shall be repaired immediately or removed from the Site. Where practical, all maintenance of equipment and vehicleson Site shall be performed off Site. If it is necessary to do maintenance outside of the designated area, the Contractor shall obtain the approval of the Project Manager or equivalentofficer prior to commencing activities. The Contractor shall ensure that in designated area andother plant maintenance facilities, including those areas where, after obtaining the Project Manager's approval, the Contractor carries out emergency plant maintenance, there is no contamination of the soil or vegetation. When servicing equipment on site, driptrays shall be used to collect the waste oil and other lubricants. Drip trays shall also be provided in construction areas for stationary plant (such as compressors) and for "parked" plant (such as scrapers, loaders, vehicles). Drip trays shall be inspectedand emptied daily. Drip trays shall be closely monitored during rain events to ensure that they do not overflow. Where practical, the Contractor shall ensure that equipment is covered so that rainwater is excluded from the drip trays. The washing of equipmentshall be restricted to urgent or preventative maintenance requirements only. All washing shall be undertaken off Site.

(xvii) **Materials stockpiles.** Material stockpiles or stacks, such as pipes, must be stable and well secured to avoid collapse and possible injury to workers or communities.

(xviii) **Toilet facilities.** A sufficient number of toilets shall be provided by the Contractor on the camp and at appropriate locations approved by the Project Manager or equivalent officer, depending on the extent of works on site. The ratio of ablution facilities to sitestaff should not exceed 1:30 and facilities shall be located within 100m from any point of work in an area approved by the Project Manager or equivalent officer. The Contractor shall ensure that no spillage occurs when toilets are cleaned or emptied and that the contents are properlystored and removed from Site. Discharge of waste from toilets into the environment is strictly prohibited.

		1 % of IPC amount will be deducted for non-compliance of any environmental safeguard requirements as mentioned in EMP.

| 4.18 | Protection of Heritage Resources | The Contractor shall take special care while performing all pre-construction, construction and post-construction activities in the heritage areas. The Contractor shall only proceed with activities until an expert-guided Heritage Impact Assessment (HIA) has been completed by the PID, and Contractor has fully understood the recommendations of the HIA and the implementation of the mitigation measures included in the EMP. Examples of activities and actions that shall be complied with by the Contractor to protect structures, sites, and sub-surface archaeology are as follows:

(i) Any subsurface paving bricks in Patan Durbar Squaredeemed of heritage value must be removed, logged and marked first before any excavation occurs so they can put placed back where they came from;
(ii) Dachhi aapa (machine made bricks) should be used for pavement;
(iii) Bedding for edge soling can be applied on lime surki sand mortar (1:1:3);
(iv) In the core zone, the excavation as noted will need to be done slowly by hand under supervision of a team of archaeologists in case of chance finds;
(v) Procedures for chance finds must be followed as outlined in the EMP and specifications;
(vi) The excavated material from the heritage site will be stacked at a different location (as mentioned in the spec.) and brought back for refilling the trench;
(vii) The contractor should employ a team of experts including archeaologist/s who have had actual experienceson excavation activities at archaeological and/or world heritage sites;
(viii) Contractor should not undertake any work without the presence of archaeologist/s as described in (vii) above;
(ix) Any other activities related to heritage compliance as instructed by the Engineer and in accordance with the EMP; and
(x) Daily Allowance for 2 Department of Archeology persons present during the supervision in the core heritage area shall be paid as per the government's norms.

Complete account of activities and actions shall be based on the results of the expert-guided HIA and EMP. As such, the Contractor shall comply with all the recommendations of the HIA and strictly implement the EMP at all times. |

ANNEX I (R): SAFEGUARD PROVISIONS IN BILL OF QUANTITY

Safeguard Items in Bill of Quantity

Summary of Cost

Part No.	Work No.	Description of Works	SHARMA-LAMA-GOLDEN GOOD JV	
			Amount in Figure (NPR)	Amount in Words (NPR)
C		**Miscellaneous Items**		
	C1	Dismantling and Reinstate of Existing Road	58,108,429.00	Fifty Eight Million One Hundred Eight Thousand Four Hundred Twenty Nine Rupees
	C2	Dismantling of existing sewerline, shoring of structure, diversion of sewage, etc.	5,222,205.00	Five Million Two Hundred Twenty Two Thousand Two Hundred Five Rupees

Bill of Quantity

Work No. A3 : Provisional Sum

Item No.	Description of Works	Unit	Quantity	Rates of SHARMA-LAMA-GOLDEN GOOD JV		Amount (NPR)
				in Figure (NPR)	in Words (NPR)	
A	**Provisional Sum for additonal Environmental Mitigation Measures, Social safe guard and Items not covered in BoQ**					
A.1	Provision for mitigation measures of unanticipated environmental impacts and social safeguard, Reinstating or relocating public utilities within land services, ie. Electric pole, transformer, street lightning, other electric line assessories, telephone poles, other telecom network infrastructures, unanticipated water supply pipe lines, water supply fittings and assessories, etc; reinstatement of affected pavement not specified in Work No. C1; reinstatement of damaged structures during construction activities, items not covered etc. including supply of necessary materials, labors, equipments, tools and installation all complete work as per specification and instructed by the Engineer.	PS	1.00	29,600,000.00	Twenty Nine Million Six Hundred Thousand Only	29,600,000.00
A.2	Supplying of potable tank water to affected area during construction works.	PS	1.00	2,400,000.00	Two Million Four Hundred Thousand Only	2,400,000.00
	Sub - Total					32,000,000.00

Part No. A: General Items, Days Works, Provisional Sum and O & M Equipment

Work No. A1 : General Items

Item No.	Description of Works	Unit	Quantity	Rates of SHARMA-LAMA-GOLDEN GOOD JV		Amount (NPR)
				in Figure (NPR)	in Words (NPR)	
C.4	Provide temporary hoardings/barricades for protection of work area with flashing lights during trench excavation in the construction site (Spec 2.6.3, see drawing in Vol. II Annex II) .	Nos.	60	30,000.00	Thirty Thousand Only	1,800,000.00
	Sub Total					6,060,000.00

Bill of Quantity

Part No. A: General Items, Days Works, Provisional Sum and O & M Equipment
Work No. A1 : General Items

Item No.	Description of Works	Unit	Quantity	Rates of SHARMA-LAMA-GOLDEN GOOD JV		Amount (NPR)
				in Figure (NPR)	in Words (NPR)	
C	EMP Implementation and Safe Guard					
C.1	Providing and installing safety signage boards, caution tapes and green nets, water sprinkling three times a day during construction works, monitoring the sound and vibrations of machine and tools, regular health check-ups in three equal time interval, trainings and awareness programs to contractor's labors, personal protective equipment, first aid kits, fire extinguishers, traffic control devices etc during construction works as per specification and engineer's instruction.. (Spec. 2.1.6) (Also refer EMP and PID safeguard manual)	months	18	100,000.00	One Hundred Thousand Only	1,800,000.00
C.2	Placement of dedicated 2 nos Safety officers throughout contract period for maintaining safety and protection against accidents including traffic control and EMP safeguard compliances with one standby emergency Vechicles. (Spec. 2.4)	months	2x18	60,000.00	Sixty Thousand Only	2,160,000.00
C.3	Placement of dedicated 1 nos Archeologist officer for 6 months period for uncovering chance findings of archelogical remains (Spec 2.4).	months	6	50,000.00	Fifty Thousand Only	300,000.00

Part No. A: General Items, Days Works, Provisional Sum and O & M Equipment
Work No. A1 : General Items

Item No.	Description of Works	Unit	Quantity	Rates of SHARMA-LAMA-GOLDEN GOOD JV		Amount (NPR)
				in Figure (NPR)	in Words (NPR)	
A	GENERAL OBLIGATIONS					
A.1	Providing and installation of project sign board of size 1.8m X 1.2m and demolishing after completion of work as per specification. (Spec 2.3.1)	Nc.s	4	20,000.00	Twenty Thousand Only	80,000.00
	Sub Total					80,000.00

Item No.	Description of Works	Unit	Quantity	Rates		Amount (NPR)
E	Temporary Walkway of steel chequered sheet (Spec 2.1.6.3)	Sqm	600	1,000.00	One Thousand Only	600,000.00
	Total Amount of WORK A1 of Part A					10,516,000.00

Part No. B: Civil Works

Work No. B1: Surface Dressing, Earthwork, Sand Filling and Other Earth Material Related Works

Item No.	Description of Works	Unit	Quantity	Rates of SHARMA-LAMA-GOLDEN GOOD JV		Amount (NPR)
				in Figure (NPR)	in Words (NPR)	
5	Providing and fixing, sheeting, struting, shoring, bracing with steel / Timber or making of trench box during trench excavation and pipe laying/ foundation works and removing after completion all complete as per drawing, specification and approval of engineer(Spec 5.2, 5.2.5.2.3, 5.2.5.2.2).	Cu m	26,464.43	200.00	Two Hundred Only	5,292,886.00
8	Loading and unloading of excavated soil materials from site to specified location (within 1km) and to site for backfilling by 3 Mt truck as per site conditions and instruction of engineer. (Spec. 11.5.10)	Cu m	11,416.28	300.00	Three Hundred Only	3,424,884.00
14	Disposal of surplus excavated earthwork materials from construction site to disposing site(within 10km premises) including loading, unloading etc. all complete. (Spec No. 11.5.10)	Cu m	6,446.34	350.00	Three Hundred Fifty Only	2,256,219.00
	Total Amount of WORK B1 of Part B					30,649,326.60

ANNEX I (S): A SAMPLE OF WORKERS CODE OF CONDUCT

All workers have a right to work in safer place with no risk to their health and safety. But workers should also follow some code of conduct to make working place safer. A sample Code of Conduct is presented hereunder.

- Comply with all laws, company policies, procedures, rules and regulations
- Cooperate with their employer on the implementation of OHS measures and other work
- Comply with instruction and cooperate with any policies and procedures related to health and safety at workplace
- Take care for their own safety and that of other person who may be affected by their work
- Use personal protective equipment at all time during work in the way they are trained and instructed
- Actively participate in health & safety training and awareness raising activities
- Follow the work procedure as oriented while performing work
- Ask with supervisor, safety officer about safety measures if not sure how to safely perform the work
- Promptly report any violations of law, accident or injury while performing work or in connection with the work
- Immediately report to their supervisor any situation which they find dangerous and also which they cannot conduct themselves
- Workers should maintain self-discipline. Do not- gamble, consume or possess drugs or alcohol in the workplace or in the camps or attend work under the influence of drugs or alcohol.
- Any person on medication or specific medication which may impair their performance must be made known to the management
- Maintain basic personal hygiene and a clean, tidy and safe working environment in and around workplace and labor camps
  - Maintaining a clean, tidy and safe working environment, free from unnecessary materials which may hamper and harm during work
  - Wash hand before eating, drinking, and as well after using the toilet
  - Careful disposal of leftover food at designated place
  - Regular cleaning of camp and work area so as not to proliferate mosquitos, flies and other vectors which may carry disease
- Reveal any circumstances with direct supervisor which may impose conflict of interest
- Report unsafe and unhealthy situation to the supervisor
- Talk to senior management of your employer, if supervisor is not solving your problem
- Do not use cell phone (except in case of emergency) and avoid playing games during working hours
- Do not invite outside visitors in the camp unless necessary
- Do not leave camp beyond allowed hours as informed by the camp in-charge
- Follow standard operating procedure such as physical distancing, use of mask and frequent hand washing using soap to prevent COVID-19 infection
- Do not involve in gender based violence, harassment or bullying at work and camp, or in the nearby settlements
- Treat and regard one another respectfully, politely and professionally at all times so as to maintain a positive working environment
- Respect the local cultures, traditions, rights etc. of the work site
- Do not involve in quarreling or crime with co-workers or in the community
- Never accept monetary favors, gifts or other considerations
- Inform visitors about the area where there are dangerous machines, chemicals or other hazardous element
- Breach of the code of conduct are considered very serious and will be dealt with stringent action that could lead to financial penalty or termination of employment/contract

ANNEX I (T): SAMPLE OF HERITAGE IMPACT ASSESSMENT STRUCTURE

ANNEX I (U): SAMPLE OF QUARTERLY PROGRESS REPORT

Kathmandu Upatyaka Khanepani Limited

Project Implementation Directorate

Anamnagar, Kathmandu, Nepal

Loan:2776-NEP

Quarterly Progress Report

January–March 2021

Implementation Agency:

Project Implementation Directorate

Prepared for	Asian Development Bank
Approved by	
Date submitted	
Date of next QPR submission	

CONTENTS

Section 1	Project Status at a Glance
Section 2	Staffing
Section 3	Contract Award and Disbursement
Section 4	Contract Management and Technical Issues
Section 5	Environmental, Social, and Occupational Health and Safety Issues
Section 6	Other Issues
Section 7	Progress on Project Outputs
Section 8	Key Implementation Issues and Status of Agreed Actions
Section 9	Compliance with Major Covenants

The Environmental Safeguards is in separate section within a chapter to be inserted in the main text of the quarterly progress report (QPR).

A. Environmental Safeguards

1. The project was environment category B. An IEE and EARF for overall project was prepared during project design and approved by ADB and GON. Individual IEE is prepared for subprojects which is .... Presented in the following table 1............

Table 1. Status of EIA/IEEs

Subproject and Contract Package	Environmental Assessment (EIA/IEE/DDR)	Status of EIA/IEE/DDR and expected date of approval	Remarks

2. A joint review of the contractor's safeguards performance was carried out with the contractors on .... during this reporting period. The result is presented in the following Table 2.

Table 2. Environmental Safeguards and OHS Performance Review

Contract Package and Contractor	Env score- %	OHS score- %	Key area of noncompliance	Agreed corrective measures in the workshop

3. The overall environmental safeguards performance of the project was rated at ..... in a scale of 100%..

B. Occupational Health and Safety

C. Compliance with Project Covenants

D. Consultation and Training

E. Recommended Corrective Actions

4. Following are the status of compliance on the corrective measures recommended during the last QPR and the measures recommended in this QPR.

   (i) Corrective actions recommended in the last QPR

Corrective Action in QPR #1, 2019	Compliance Status	Remark

   (ii) Corrective actions recommended by this QPR

   ▪
   ▪
   ▪

ANNEX II: MONITORING FORMS

ANNEX II: MONITORING FORMS

SN	Detail	Stage to Use the Form	Type of Work	Infrastructure
1	Site Inspection Form #211 A	Joint Monitoring with Contractor before Field Mobilization	Confined Area	Service Reservoir Tank
2	Monitoring Score Sheet #211 B	Joint Monitoring and Performance Scoring during Construction	Confined Area	Service Reservoir Tank (Confined Area)
3	Site Inspection Form #212 A	Joint Monitoring with Contractor before Field Mobilization	Linear Alignment	Bulk Distribution and DNI
4	Monitoring Score Sheet #212 B	Joint Monitoring and Performance Scoring during Construction	Linear Alignment	Bulk Distribution and DNI
5	Monitoring Score Sheet #212 C	Joint Monitoring and Performance Scoring during Construction	Linear Alignment	Chamber/ Manhole/ Interconnection/ Pressure Test/ Butterfly Valve in WS (Work in Linear Alignment)
6	Commissioning Monitoring Form #212 D	Joint Monitoring and Performance Scoring during Commissioning for WS System	Both confined and linear work	BDS including SRT/ DNI
7	Stockyard Monitoring Form #212 E	Joint Monitoring and Performance Scoring during Construction	Both confined and linear work	BDS/DNI/TP/SN/IS/ During Construction
8	Site Inspection Form #213 A	Joint Monitoring with Contractor before Field Mobilization	Linear work	Sewer Network/ Interceptor Network
9	Monitoring Score Sheet #213 B	Joint Monitoring and Performance Scoring during Construction	Linear work	Sewer Network/ Interceptor Network
11	Site Inspection Form #214 A	Joint Monitoring with Contractor before Field Mobilization	Confined area	Wastewater Treatment Plant
12	Monitoring Score Sheet #214 B	Joint Monitoring and Performance Scoring during Construction	Confined area	Wastewater Treatment Plant
13	Environmental Audit Checklist #215	Generally, upon completion of work and operation for a year or two		BDS/ DNI/ SN/ IS/ WWTP
14	Labor Camp Monitoring Checklist#216	Labor Camp Monitoring Checklist during construction	Both main camp and site camps	All types
15	Accident/Injury Report Form #217	During construction and operation		All types
16	Grievance Redress Mechanism Schematic Diagram #218	Planning, implementation and operation all stages		All types
17	Heritage Impact Assessment/Chance Find Procedure Form #219	Chance Find Procedure while working at ancient or heritage areas for planning and implementation stages		All types

Kathmandu Upatyaka Khanepani Limited

Project Implementation Directorate

SITE INSPECTION FORM #211 A

Joint Monitoring with Contractor before Field Mobilization

Service Reservoir Tank

(confined area)

Purpose:	Review contractor's EMP/SEMP compliance preparations before field mobilization
Frequency:	Once before field mobilization and follow-up monitoring using monitoring checklist #212 B
Stage:	Contract awarded. Before field mobilization the contractor submits SEMP for approval
Responsible:	Project staff/engineer and contractor's staff (PM, safeguard, and safety staff)- jointly

Date:		Time:	

Project Detail

Contract package:	Weather (√):
Name of contractor:	
Name of site in-charge:	Municipality:
Name of safeguard/safety staff and others with contact no:	Ward No: Tole:
1.	3.
2.	4.

Technical Detail

Site area:	Soil Type* (√): A B C
Proposed structures:	
Site topography (√): (i) Flat (ii) Rolling	

Land use (√)	Urban	Peri-urban	Rural	Heritage	Agri	Forest	Riverside

Drainage condition and probability of flooding:		
Date to start construction:	Date to complete construction:	
SEMP/OHS Approved (√): Y N	Submission date:	Approval date:

Issues:

SN	Issues	Y/N/NA	Remarks
Upfront activities:			
1	Have all approvals/ permits from the government been obtained? Any pending approvals with planned date?		
2	Are there any land acquisition related issue. If yes, what is the status (compensation, deed transfer)?		

SN	Issues	Y/N/NA	Remarks
3	Is the site accessible? Any traffc-related issue? If yes, coordination with traffic police?		
4	Are there underground facility, overhead transmission line, or heritage area- related issue? What is the plan?		
5	Is community informed of the work? Are there any community concern? Any response by the project?		
6	Are their any sensitive receivers around the site. List?		
7	Has contractor mobilized safeguard officer and safety officer? Was their CV approved by engineer?		
SEMP and OHS implementation arrangements (maps, resources, tools, and facilities):			
1	Site base map of camp facilities and sensitive receptors prepared		
2	Site delineated, cleaned, fenced, and arrangements for guarding and lighting prepared		
3	Plan to establish camp with cabins, kitchen, dinning, toilet (male and female), water supply, waste management, recreational facility, etc. at required standard prepared		
	Arrangements for health and safety of workers along with medical room, health worker, first aid, fire extinguisher, and emergency protocol considered in the OHS plan		
4	Safety and informative signboards designed (in local language) as per PID standards		
5	On-site manual and vehicular movement path designated on the map		
6	Plantation plan with nursery prepared for tree, garden, and greening of the area		
7	Construction material stockpile and chemicals storage area identified and demarcated		
8	Topsoil collection, and excavated material stockpile area arranged		
9	Waste management system established		
10	Arrangement for air, water, noise level test and location finalized in reference to sensitive receptors		
11	Proper landscaping and drainage plan prepared		
12	Workers code of conduct prepared and approved		
13	EMP and OHS compliance monitoring checklist prepared		
14	Contractor's routine reporting format and frequency agreed in SEMP		

SN	Issues	Y/N/NA	Remarks
Other issues if any?			
Any Particular Remark:			

Signature	Signature	Signature
Name and Position	**Name and Position**	**Name and Position**

Note:

* Soil Type:

Type A soil is the most stable soil in which to excavate. Examples of type A soil include clay, silty clay, sandy clay, and clay loam.

Type B soil is cohesive and has often been cracked or disturbed. It has medium unconfined compressive strength. Examples of Type B soil include angular gravel, silt, silt loam, and soils that are fissured or near sources of vibration, but could otherwise be Type A.

Type C soil is the least stable soil. It is cohesive and has a high unconfined compressive strength. It includes granular soils in which particles do not stick together and cohesive soils with a low unconfined compressive strength. Examples of Type C soil include gravel and sand.

Detailed Site Plan (sketch) with Structure Location and Sensitive Receptor

NOTE: Refer to Section- for the guidelines and instructions required for a site plan map

Kathmandu Upatyaka Khanepani Limited
Project Implementation Directorate
MONITORING SCORE SHEET #211 B
Joint Monitoring and Performance Scoring during Construction

Service Reservoir Tank

(confined area)

Purpose:	Review contractor's EMP/SEMP compliance performance during work implementation
Frequency:	Daily/once a week (as required) when work is ongoing
Stage:	Construction stage and when work is ongoing at the particular site

Responsible: Project staff/environment expert of engineer and contractor's staff (PM, safeguard, and safety staff)- jointly

Date:	Time:

Project Detail

Contract package:	Weather (√):
Name of contractor:	
Name of site in-charge:	Municipality:
Name of safeguard/safety staff and others with contact no:	Ward No: Tole:
1.	3.
2.	4.

Workers

Number of workers (number):	Female:	Male:	Child:

SN	Item	Activities	Yes (√)	No (√)	Full Score	Score Card	Corrective Action Agreed with Deadline
1		Work implemented only when the site engineer/ supervisor and safety officer is present at site.			2		
		Camp structure constructed, and facilities is provided as per the PID standard attached to CA. No tarpaulin tents are used.			6		
		Few ready-made tents at stock to use for isolation in case of emergency such as COVID-19 infection.			1		
		% of workers using full set of PPEs (hard hat, reflective jacket, gloves, goggles, boot, face mask, safety belt etc.			3		
		Site fenced, guarded, people registered at entry in camp.			2		

SN	Item	Activities	Yes (√)	No (√)	Full Score	Score Card	Corrective Action Agreed with Deadline
	Occupational Health and Safety	Site landscaped with proper drainage system. No water pools in the site.			2		
		Separate movement path for people and vehicles clearly demarked inside the site.			2		
		First aid box at site at all time. Group leader trained in using the first aid.			2		
		Medical room with full-time health worker arranged. Required emergency supplies and sick bed available, as well as standby vehicle in case of emergency.			4		
		Emergency contact person name and number pasted in the camp and available with workers.			1		
		Emergency assembly point demarcated?			1		
		Health of workers screened during intake, and periodic health check-up conducted (twice a year).			2		
		Fire extinguisher available at site and camp and workers trained to use them.			2		
		Double insulated wire used at work areas and camp.			3		
		Clean and hard safety barricades used at site.			5		
		Shoring done in trenches (trench > 1 meter depth).			5		
		Construction material kept at minimum 2 meter distance away from trench.			2		
		Guard rail and three board working platform arranged during work at height.			5		
		Construction materials (cement, aggregate, rebar, scaffolding, formwork, fuel and lubricant) and waste stockpiled properly at designated location.			3		
		Operational procedure for use of construction equipment is prepared and provided to worker.			2		
		Site area/path is clean of nail, rods, bricks, and other sharp materials for safety of workers.			3		
		Chemical and fuel stored properly (impervious platform with drain/sump well, spill kit available).			2		
		Cement slurry, chemicals, and/or oils are not discharged over the ground.			2		

SN	Item	Activities	Yes (√)	No (√)	Full Score	Score Card	Corrective Action Agreed with Deadline
2	Noise, Air, and Water Quality	Noise level monitored at agreed frequency.			2		
		Earplug used by workers at noisy area.			2		
		Drinking water supplied at camp and work site tested at agreed frequency.			2		
		Water reserved for 48 hours at all time.			2		
		Volumetric air sampler placed near sensitive receptor and measured at required intervals.			2		
		Proper water sprinkling done to suppress dust.			4		
3	Signage	Standard signboard for safety, SOP, traffic prepared as per PID standards and placed at right location.			2		
4	Community Safety	Safety Desk at site and operational.			3		
		Grievance register kept at site and office.			2		
		Common access road kept clean of potholes and dust if used by project vehicle.			2		
5	Solid Waste	Solid waste at camp and work area properly segregated and disposed. Burning is restricted.			3		
6	Sanitation Facilities	Sufficient number of toilet and bath with water arranged .			2		
		Separate toilet provided for male/female.			2		
		Toilet wastes discharged into septic tank.			2		
		Bathing/washing/cooking water discharged into sewer or septic tank after storing in collection pit.			2		
		Separate kitchen and dining provided. No cooking and eating inside cabins.			2		
		Drainage management at the site.			2		
		TOTAL			100		
		TOTAL (%)					

Note:

1. If the work is being done in confined space, then confined space checklist needs to be filled.

2. Assign points of high importance to certain "Activities" and if even half score is not met for those points, the total scoring could be considered as not met the requirement even if all the other points are met.

On behalf of PID and Consultant	On behalf of the contractor
Name and Position:	**Name and Position:**
Signature:	**Signature:**
Date:	**Date:**

Kathmandu Upatyaka Khanepani Limited

Project Implementation Directorate

SITE INSPECTION FORM #212 A

Joint Monitoring with Contractor before Field Mobilization

Bulk Distribution and Distribution Network Improvement

(linear work)

Purpose:	Review contractor's EMP/SEMP compliance preparations before field mobilization
Frequency:	Once before field mobilization and follow-up monitoring using monitoring checklist #212B
Stage:	Contract awarded. Before field mobilization, the contractor submits SEMP for approval.
Responsible:	Project staff/engineer and contractor's staff (PM, safeguard, and safety staff)- jointly

Date:	Time:

Project Detail

Contract package:	Weather (√):
Name of contractor:	
Name of site in-charge:	Municipality:
Name of safeguard/safety staff and others with contact no:	Ward No: Tole:
1.	3.
2.	4.

Technical Detail

Site area:	Soil Type* (√): A B C

Proposed structures:	

Site topography (√): (i) Flat (ii) Rolling	

Land use (√)	Urban	Peri-urban	Rural	Heritage	Agri	Forest	Riverside

Drainage condition and probability of flooding:	

Date to start construction:	Date to complete construction:

SEMP/OHS Approved (√): Y N	Submission date:	Approval date:

Issues:			
SN	**Issues**	**Y/N/NA**	**Remarks**
Upfront activities are in place			
1	Are the critical sites along the alignment are identified, SEMP and OHS prepared, and consulted with local community and administration?		
2	Is the construction site clear and secure?		
3	Any land acquisition-related issue are resolved?		

SN	Issues	Y/N/NA	Remarks
4	Are the sensitive receivers along the alignment identified?		
5	Are the underground utilities, overhead transmission line, and work in heritage area identified?		
6	Does the pipeline pass through sidewalk, footpath, crossing, river crossing, etc.? Mention locations.		
7	Have all approvals/permits from the government been. obtained? Any pending approvals with planned date?		
8	Procedure for excavation of trench (zero soil concept), pipelaying, backfilling, and resurfacing procedure submitted and approved by engineer?		
9	Are the community informed of the work details? Are there any community concern? Are they addressed?		
10	Is access to the alignment clear?		
11	Is working in night shift proposed? Any issue?		
12	Has contractor appointed safeguard staff and safety officer?		
SEMP and OHS implementation arrangements (maps, resources, tools, and facilities):			
1	Arrangement made for traffic management, diversion and information board placed at entry and exit points of lane in coordination with public, ward and traffic police.		
2	Chequered plate arranged for pedestrian crossing over trench.		
3	Has pipe stockpile area and temporary soil stockpile area at site identified and approved by the local government and the engineer and agreed by the community?		
4	Proper procedure for stacking pipes, loading, and unloading at site prepared?		
5	Location for labor camp identified and approved by local government and engineer? No conflict with community?		
6	Plan to establish camp with cabins, kitchen, dinning, toilet (male and female), water supply, waste management, recreational facility, etc. at required standard prepared.		
7	Type of safety barricade and covering net for pipe trench and manholes approved by engineer? Arrangements made for supply of required specification of barricades before work begins?		
8	Labor camp construction initiated following the PID standards. No site camp to be established, to the extent possible. If needed, are readymade tents arranged?		
9	Arrangements made for health and safety of workers along with medical room, health worker, first aid, fire extinguisher, and emergency protocol at camp and work site?		

SN	Issues	Y/N/NA	Remarks
10	Safety and informative sign boards designed (in local language) as per PID standards?		
11	Vegetation plantation plan prepared for planting trees from the site and greening of the area?		
12	Health and safety plan (OHS) for staff and workers prepared?		
13	Proper waste management system at camp established?		
14	Arrangement for air, water, noise level test at sensitive location for test finalized and approved by engineer?		
15	Recordkeeping system for damages in private and social utilities and structures, and procedure to reinstate them with deadline is prepared?		
16	Workers code of conduct prepared and approved?		
17	Is there any provision for employing local people in the construction activities?		
18	Are there any complaints from the neighborhood regarding the alignment of pipe?		
19	EMP and OHS compliance monitoring checklist prepared?		
	Workers health screening and routine monitoring system established?		
20	Contractor's routine reporting format and frequency agreed in SEMP?		
Other issues if any?			
Any Particular Remark:			

Signature	Signature	Signature
Name and Position	**Name and Position**	**Name and Position**

Note:

* Soil Type:

Type A soil is the most stable soil in which to excavate. Examples of type A soil include clay, silty clay, sandy clay, and clay loam.

Type B soil is cohesive and has often been cracked or disturbed. It has medium unconfined compressive strength. Examples of Type B soil include angular gravel, silt, silt loam, and soils that are fissured or near sources of vibration, but could otherwise be Type A.

Type C soil is the least stable soil. It is cohesive and has a high unconfined compressive strength. It includes granular soils in which particles do not stick together and cohesive soils with a low unconfined compressive strength. Examples of Type C soil include gravel and sand.

Detailed Site Plan (sketch) with Sewer Alignment and Sensitive Receptors

Kathmandu Upatyaka Khanepani Limited

Project Implementation Directorate

MONITORING SCORE SHEET #212 B

Joint Monitoring and Performance Scoring during Construction

Bulk Distribution and Distribution Network Improvement

(linear work)

Purpose:	Review contractor's EMP/SEMP compliance performance during work implementation
Frequency:	Daily/once a week (as required) when work is ongoing
Stage:	Construction stage and when work is ongoing at the particular site
Responsible:	Project staff/environment expert of engineer and contractor's staff (PM, safeguard, and safety staff)-jointly

Date:		Time:	
Project Detail			
Contract package:		Weather (√):	
Name of contractor:			
Name of site in-charge:		Municipality:	
Name of safeguard/safety staff and others with contact no:		Ward No: Tole:	
1.		3.	
2.		4.	
Workers			
Number of workers (number):	Female:	Male:	Child:

SN	Item	Activities	Yes (√)	No (√)	Full Mark	Score	Corrective Action Agreed with Deadline
1	Occupational Health and Safety	Work implemented only when the site engineer/supervisor and safety officer is present at site.			2		
		Camp structure constructed, and facilities is provided as per the PID standard attached to CA. No tarpaulin tents are used.			4		
		Few readymade tents at stock to use for isolation in case of emergency such as COVID-19 infection.			2		
		Health of workers screened during intake, and periodic health check-up conducted (twice a year).			2		
		% of workers using full set of PPEs (hard hat, reflective jacket, gloves, goggles, boot, face mask, safety belt, etc.)			3		

SN	Item	Activities	Yes (√)	No (√)	Full Mark	Score	Corrective Action Agreed with Deadline
		Camp site fenced and guarded.			2		
		Work site hard barricaded and unauthorized people prevented from getting close to work area.			4		
		First aid box at site at all time. Group leader trained in using the first aid.			2		
		Medical room with full-time health worker arranged. Required emergency supplies and sick bed available, as well as standby vehicle in case of emergency.			4		
		Emergency contact person name and number available with workers.			1		
		Clean drinking water is available at work site.			2		
		Mobile and moveable PVC toilet provided at site. Toilet of local residents shall not be used.			2		
		Shoring done in trenches as per design.			3		
2	Noise, Air, Water Quality	Water spraying done at regular intervals (3-4 times a day) to suppress dust but not create water pool and mud as instructed by the engineer and temporary sealing applied.			4		
		Noise level measurement placed near sensitive receptors at agreed frequency.			2		
		Tested and clean water supplied to work sites.			3		
3	Access without Obstruction; Housekeeping in work area	Steel plate to cross trench of BDS and DNI Pipeline by public is available at site.			4		
		Depending on road/lane width, half portion is left clean and open for traffic during construction.			4		
		Keep trench length not more than a pipe length or 30 meters and backfilled on the same day.			3		
		Are pipes stored and properly stacked at designated location near the site and not at the work location causing visual nuisance? Safety during loading and unloading properly followed?			3		
		Are construction materials covered while transporting and storing?			3		
		Standby truck or tractor carries the excavated and excess soil immediately upon excavation for proper storage and disposal at approved location (zero soil concept).			5		

SN	Item	Activities	Yes (√)	No (√)	Full Mark	Score	Corrective Action Agreed with Deadline
		Wheelbarrow used to carry the excavated and excess soil at the site in narrow lanes where no access to trucks.			5		
		Is the material stored safely without causing load on trench wall and make them cave or material falling in the trench?			2		
		Construction materials (aggregates, unused and damaged pipes, signage board) removed after laying pipe, backfilling, and compaction.			5		
		Excess soil is not disposed at the waterbodies.			3		
4	Signage	Standard signboard for safety, SOP information used as per PID standard and placed at required locations.			3		
		Proper traffic diversion signboard used as per PID standard and placed at required location with priority at entry and exit points of a lane.			3		
5	GRM	Safety Desk at site and operational.			3		
		Grievance register kept at site and office.			3		
6	Damaged Utilities Repairs	Availability of recordkeeping system for damages in private and community infrastructure services/ utilities.			2		
		Repair of damaged social utilities (within agreed period–generally 2 days). Alternative arrangement made.			4		
		Backfilling and compacting of trench the same day after completion of work. Temporary sealing of blacktop or concrete road within 2 days .			3		
	TOTAL				100		
	TOTAL (%)						

Note: Assign points of high importance to certain "Activities" and if even half score is not met for those points, the total scoring could be considered as not met the requirement even if all the other points are met.

On behalf of PID and Consultant	**On behalf of the contractor**
Name and Position:	**Name and Position:**
Signature:	**Signature:**
Date:	**Date:**

Kathmandu Upatyaka Khanepani Limited

Project Implementation Directorate

MONITORING SCORE SHEET #212 C

Joint Monitoring and Performance Scoring during Construction

Chamber/ Manhole/Interconnection/ Pressure Test/ Butterfly Valve in Water Supply

(linear work)

Purpose:	Review contractor's EMP/SEMP compliance performance during work implementation
Frequency:	Daily/once a week (as required) when work is ongoing
Stage:	Construction stage and when work is ongoing at the particular site
Responsible:	Project staff/environment expert of engineer and contractor's staff (PM, safeguard, and safety staff)-jointly

Date:	Time:

Project Detail

Contract package:	Weather (√):
Name of contractor:	
Name of site in-charge:	Municipality:
Name of safeguard/safety staff and others with contact no:	Ward No: Tole:
1.	3.
2.	4.

Workers

Number of workers (number):	Female:	Male:	Child:

SN	Item	Activities	Yes (√)	No (√)	Full Score	Score Card	Corrective Action Agreed with Deadline
1	Occupational Health and Safety	Work implemented only when the site engineer/ supervisor and safety officer is present at site.			4		
		% of workers using full set of PPEs (hard hat, reflective jacket, gloves, goggles, boot, face mask, safety belt, etc.).			8		
		Work site has hard barricade for manhole/ chamber: zinc sheet height 1.22 meters and width as per the width of the chamber.			10		
		Metal posts available both vertically and horizontally, so that no vehicles can accidently fall inside the chamber.			10		
		First aid box at site at all time. Group leader trained in using first aid.			4		

SN	Item	Activities	Yes (√)	No (√)	Full Score	Score Card	Corrective Action Agreed with Deadline
		Clean drinking water is available at work site.			4		
		Emergency contact person name and number available with workers.			2		
		Reflective tape available all around the chamber to make it visible at night.			10		
		Excess soil, construction materials (aggregates, unused & damaged pipes, signage board) removed immediately (zero soil concept).			10		
		Mobile and moveable PVC toilet provided at site. Toilet of local residents shall not be used.			4		
		Backfilling and compaction done on the same day after completion of work.			10		
2	Signage	Standard signboard for safety, SOP information, and work start and completion date placed as per PID standard and placed at required locations.			10		
		Proper traffic diversion signboard used as per PID standard and placed at required location.			8		
3	GRM	Safety desk at site and operational.			3		
		Grievance register kept at site and office.			3		
	TOTAL (%)				**100**		

Note: Assign points of high importance to certain "Activities" and if even half score is not met for those points, the total scoring could be considered as not met the requirement even if all the other points are met.

On behalf of PID and Consultant	On behalf of the contractor
Name and Position:	**Name and Position:**
Signature:	**Signature:**
Date:	**Date:**

Kathmandu Upatyaka Khanepani Limited
Project Implementation Directorate
COMMISSIONING MONITORING FORM #212 D
Joint Monitoring and Performance Scoring during Construction

Place:	Date:

Purpose:	Environmental compliance performance during commissioning of the system
Frequency:	During commissioning
Stage:	Commissioning stage
Responsible:	Project staff/environment expert of engineer and contractor's staff (PM, safeguard, and safety staff)- jointly

Date:	Time:

Project Detail

Contract package:	Weather (√):
Name of contractor:	
Name of site in-charge:	Municipality:
Name of safeguard/safety staff and others with contact no:	Ward No: Tole:
1.	3.
2.	4.

Workers

Number of workers (number):	Female:	Male:	Child:

SN	Subject	Activities	Yes/No/NA	Remarks
1	Signage	Project information board placed at the site.		
		Safety awareness board placed at site.		
		Traffic diversion information placed at site.		
2	Communication and information dissemination and emergency preparedness	Permit taken to work in confined space and with deep excavation.		
		Prior information provided to all residents on schedule of meter installation, checking, and flow monitoring and associated risks.		
		Traffic police and ward office informed of activity, location, and schedule.		
		Miking carried out focusing on risk-prone (high-pressure) areas to keep the community informed of the scheduled commissioning.		

SN	Subject	Activities	Yes/No/NA	Remarks
		Rescue arrangements at place at all the high-pressure critical points in case of emergency.		
		Mobilization of a standby team to continuously check/monitor leakages at lines and valves.		
		Communication system between the operator and the monitoring team is established in case immediate closure of water supply is needed due to high leakage, joint failure, and rupture.		
		Interagency communication system established between the PID, NEA, DOR, KUKL, and municipalities and their contact number with responsible authority is available at site in case of pipe rupture.		
		Standby machinery (backhoe loader and 10-ton roller) is available 24x7 for all types of "rescue" in case of any event.		
3.	Occupational Health and Safety	Damaged site barricaded with hard barricade, warning signs and reflective tape.		
		Workers and all team used full PPEs (along with oxygen mask, full sleeve vest, boot, face shield especially during high-dose disinfection).		
		First Aid box available at the site.		
		Help desk and grievance register at the site.		
		Drinking water arranged at the site.		
		Good housekeeping is maintained at the commissioning site.		
		Gas detection done before high dose disinfection test.		
		All monitoring, working team and community were informed to stay at safe distance from the pipeline/chamber.		
		Clearance of the area of influence after proper backfill, compaction and repair.		
4	Documentation and reporting	Reporting of procedure adopted and activity detail including any emergency measures required to be taken.		
5	Certification	Successful commissioning is certified by the engineer.		

On behalf of PID and consultant	On behalf of the contractor
Name:	Name:
Signature:	Signature:
Date:	Date:
Mobile No:	Mobile No:

Kathmandu Upatyaka Khanepani Limited

Project Implementation Directorate

STOCKYARD MONITORING FORM #212 E

Joint Monitoring and Performance Scoring during Construction

Place:		Date:

Purpose:	Review contractor's EMP/SEMP compliance performance during work implementation
Frequency:	Once in two weeks (as required) when work is on-going
Stage:	Construction Stage and when work is on-going at the particular site
Responsible:	Project Staff/Environment Expert of Engineer and Contractor's staff (PM, safeguard, and safety staff)- Jointly

Project Detail

Contract package:	Weather (√):
Name of contractor:	
Name of site in-charge:	Municipality:
Name of Safeguard/Safety Staff and others with contact no:	Ward No: Tole:
1.	3.
2.	4.

Workers

Number of workers (number):	Female:	Male:	Child:

SN	Subject	Activities	Yes/No/NA	Remarks
1.	Material handling procedure	A procedure for handling, loading, unloading, stacking and record keeping is prepared for managing construction materials stockyard		
2.	Information dissemination	Signboards displaying information of project, no entry signs, danger sign, and no smoking sign placed at appropriate locations (at stock yard, in front of the gate, in front of diesel/petrol and oil and inflammable chemical storage areas)		
3.	Piling of stocks- pipes, fittings and construction aggregates	All material & equipment are placed at delineated area as shown in the layout map		
		The pipes are properly piled at stockyard		
		The fittings are placed separately and neatly with inventory system		

SN	Subject	Activities	Yes/No/NA	Remarks
4.	Housekeeping	Drainage is maintained around stockyard		
		The road at the stockyard area are clean and dry at all times		
		The unwanted scrapes and metals are disposed at designated area with barricade		
		All waste and unusable material collected and disposed as per waste management plan		
5.	Placing of chemicals (lubricants, petrol/diesel)	Spill kits i.e. extra bucket, sand, full body PPE, sponges etc. placed at chemical storage area		
		Team of staff and worker handling such material will be a group of well trained persons		
		The store/yard is at least 300 ft away from camp and work sites		
6.	Electrical Safety	Use of double insulated wire		
		Use of three pin cord		
7.	Safety protocol	Emergency assembly point is designated		
		First aid box and medical room are kept ready for emergency situation		
		Workers have name and phone number of the safety officer and site in-charge to report incase of emergency situation		
		Understanding with nearest hospital made for emergency call and vehicle ready to transport injured to the hospital		

On behalf of PID and consultant	On behalf of the contractor
Name:	Name:
Signature:	Signature:
Date:	Date:
Mobile No:	Mobile No:

Kathmandu Upatyaka Khanepani Limited

Project Implementation Directorate

SITE INSPECTION FORM #213 A

Joint Monitoring with Contractor before Field Mobilization

Sewer Network/Interceptor Network

(linear work)

Purpose:	Review contractor's EMP/SEMP compliance preparations before field mobilization
Frequency:	Once before field mobilization and follow-up monitoring using monitoring checklist #212B
Stage:	Contract awarded. Before field mobilization the contractor submits SEMP for approval.
Responsible:	Project staff/engineer and contractor's staff (PM, safeguard, and safety staff)- jointly
Date:	Time:

Project Detail

Contract package:		Weather (√) :	
Name of contractor:			
Name of site in-charge:		Municipality:	
Name of safeguard/safety staff and others with contact no:		Ward No: Tole:	
1.		3.	
2.		4.	

Site Area:	Soil Type* (√): A B C	
Proposed structures:		
Site topography (√): (i) Flat (ii) Rolling		

Land use (√)	Urban	Peri-urban	Rural	Heritage	Agri	Forest	Riverside

Drainage condition and probability of flooding:		
Date to start construction:	Date to complete construction:	
SEMP/OHS Approved (√): Y N	Submission date:	Approval date:

Technical Details

Name of the project:		
Excavation width :	Excavation Length:	Excavation Depth:
Soil classification:	Type A ( ) Type B ( )	Type C ( )
Type of protective system to be used:		

Total design length of the sewer pipe till the treatment plant:	
Design capacity of sewer pipe:	
Date of construction to be started:	

Issues			
SN	**Issues**	**Yes/No/NA**	**Remarks**
Upfront activities are in place			
1	Are the critical sites along the alignment identified, SEMP and OHS prepared, and local community and administration consulted?		
2	Is the construction site clear and secure?		
3	Are all the land acquisition-related issues resolved?		
4	Are the sensitive receivers along the alignment identified?		
5	Are the underground utilities, overhead transmission line, and work in heritage area identified?		
6	Does the pipeline pass through sidewalk, footpath, crossing, river crossing, etc. Mention locations.		
7	Have all approvals/permits from the government been obtained? Any pending approvals with planned date?		
8	Procedure for excavation of trench (zero soil concept), pipelaying, backfilling, and resurfacing procedure submitted and approved by the engineer?		
9	Are the community informed of the work details? Are there any community concern? Are they addressed?		
10	Is access to the alignment clear?		
11	Is working in night shift proposed? Any issue?		
12	Has contractor appointed safeguard staff and safety officer?		
SEMP and OHS implementation arrangements (maps, resources, tools, and facilities)			
1	Has pipe stockpile area and temporary soil stockpile area at site identified and approved by the local government and the engineer and agreed by the community?		
2	Is the procedure for material loading, unloading, stacking, and handling prepared?		
3	Location for labor camp identified and approved by the local government and the engineer? No conflict with community?		

SN	Issues	Yes/No/NA	Remarks
4	Is plan to establish camp with cabins, kitchen, dinning, toilet (male and female), water supply, waste management, recreational facility, etc. at required standard prepared?		
5	Is type of safety barricade and covering net for pipe trench and manholes approved by the engineer? Arrangements made for supply of required specification of barricades before work begins?		
6	Is labor camp construction initiated following the PID standards. No site camp to be established, to the extent possible. If needed, are readymade tents arranged?		
7	Are arrangements made for the health and safety of workers along with medical room, health worker, first aid, fire extinguisher, and emergency protocol at camp and work site?		
8	Are safety and informative sign boards designed (in local language) as per PID standards?		
9	Is vegetation plantation plan prepared for planting trees from the site and greening of the area?		
10	Is health and safety plan for staff and workers prepared?		
11	Is proper waste management system at camp established?		
12	Is arrangement for air, water, noise level test at sensitive location for test finalized and approved by the engineer?		
13	Is plan for minimizing air, water, and noise pollution due to the construction activities prepared?		
14	Is workers code of conduct prepared and approved?		
15	Is there any provision for employing local people in the construction activities?		
16	Are there any complaints from the neighborhood regarding the alignment of pipe?		
17	Are EMP and OHS compliance monitoring checklists prepared?		
18	Are contractor's routine reporting format and frequency agreed in the SEMP?		

Other issues if any?

Note:

* Soil Type:

Type A soil is the most stable soil in which to excavate. Examples of type A soil include clay, silty clay, sandy clay, and clay loam.

Type B soil is cohesive and has often been cracked or disturbed. It has medium unconfined compressive strength. Examples of Type B soil include angular gravel, silt, silt loam, and soils that are fissured or near sources of vibration, but could otherwise be Type A.

Type C soil is the least stable soil. It is cohesive and has a high unconfined compressive strength. It includes granular soils in which particles do not stick together and cohesive soils with a low unconfined compressive strength. Examples of Type C soil include gravel and sand.

Field Site Sketch And Cross-Sections (Site Plan)

Kathmandu Upatyaka Khanepani Limited

Project Implementation Directorate

MONITORING SCORE SHEET#213 B

Joint Monitoring and Performance Scoring during Construction

Sewer Network/Interceptor Network

(linear work)

Purpose:	Review contractor's EMP/SEMP compliance performance during work implementation
Frequency:	Daily/once a week (as required) when work is ongoing
Stage:	Construction stage and when work is ongoing at the particular site
Responsible:	Project staff/environment expert of engineer and contractor's staff (PM, safeguard, and safety staff)-jointly
Date:	Time:

Project Detail

Contract package:	Weather (√):
Name of contractor:	
Name of site in-charge:	Municipality:
Name of safeguard/safety staff and others with contact no:	Ward No: Tole:
1.	3.
2.	4.

Workers

Number of workers (number):	Female:	Male:	Child:

SN	Item	Activities	Yes (√)	No (√)	Full Mark	Score	Corrective Action Agreed with Deadline
1		Work implemented only when the site engineer/ supervisor and safety officer is present at site.			2		
		Camp structure constructed, and facilities are provided as per the PID standard attached to the CA. No tarpaulin tents are used.			4		
		Few readymade tents at stock to use for isolation in case of emergency such as the COVID-19 infection.			2		
		Health of workers screened during intake, and periodic health check-up (twice a year).			2		
		% of workers using full set of PPEs (hard hat, reflective jacket, gloves, goggles, boot, face mask, safety belt, etc.) .			3		

SN	Item	Activities	Yes (√)	No (√)	Full Mark	Score	Corrective Action Agreed with Deadline
	Occupational Health and Safety	Use of PPEs (hard hat and reflective jacket) by site engineer/supervisor/safety officer whenever they enter site.			2		
		Camp site fenced and guarded.			2		
		Work site hard barricaded (minimum 4-feet height) and unauthorized people prevented from getting close to the work area.			4		
		First aid box at site at all time. Group leader trained in using first aid.			2		
		Medical room with full-time health worker arranged. Required emergency supplies and sick bed available. Standby vehicle in case of emergency.			4		
		Emergency contact person name and number available with workers.			1		
		Clean drinking water is available at the work site.			2		
		Mobile and movable PVC toilet provided at site. Use of toilet of local residents is restricted.			2		
		Shoring done in trenches as per design.			3		
2	Noise, Air, Water Quality	Water sprinkle at regular intervals (3-4 times a day) as instructed by the engineer and apply temporary bituminous sealing.			4		
		Noise level measurement near sensitive receptors at agreed frequency.			2		
		If the sewer crosses river, proper measure taken not to deposit excavated soil from river bed at work area or as instructed by the engineer, and not to increase sediment load in river. Such crossings are protected by gabion weir on top of the pipe.			3		
		Tested and clean water supplied to work sites .			3		
3	Access without obstruction	Iron chequered plates are available to put on trench for crossing by pedestrians.			3		
		Depending on road/lane width, half portion is left clean and open for traffic during construction.			3		
		Keep trench length not more than a pipe length or 30 meters and backfilled on the same day.			3		
		Are pipes stored and properly stacked at site?			3		

SN	Item	Activities	Yes (√)	No (√)	Full Mark	Score	Corrective Action Agreed with Deadline
		Are construction materials covered while transporting and storing?			3		
		Standby truck or tractor carries the excavated and excess soil for proper storage/disposal at approved location (zero soil concept).			4		
		Wheelbarrow used to carry the excavated and excess soil at the site in narrow lanes where no access to trucks.			4		
		Is the material stored safely without causing load on trench wall and make them cave or material falling in trench?			2		
		Construction materials (aggregates, unused and damaged pipes, signage board) removed after laying pipe, backfilling, and compaction.			4		
		Pipes stored and stacked at designated location near the site. Are construction materials covered with tarpaulin.			2		
		Excess soil is not disposed into waterbodies.			2		
4	Signage	Standard signboard for safety, SOP information used as per the PID standard and placed at required locations.			2		
		Proper traffic diversion signboard used as per the PID standard and placed at required location with priority at entry and exit points of a lane.			3		
5	GRM	Safety Help Desk at site and operational.			2		
		Grievance register kept at site and office.			2		
		Any complaint of noise and air, access by locals? Are they addressed.			2		
6	Damaged Utilities Repairs	Availability of record keeping system for damages in private and community infrastructure services/ utilities .			2		
		Repair of damaged social utilities (within agreed period, generally 2 days). Alternative arrangement made.			3		
		Backfilling and compacting of trench the same day after completion of work. Temporary sealing of blacktop or concrete road within 2 days.			2		
		Potable tank of water supplied to the affected houses during the time of construction and excavation of trenches when water supply pipe might be disrupted.			2		
	TOTAL				100		
	TOTAL (%)						

Note: Assign points of high importance to certain "Activities" and if even half score is not met for those points, the total scoring could be considered as not met the requirement even if all the other points are met.

On behalf of PID and Consultant	On behalf of the contractor
Name and Position:	Name and Position:
Signature:	Signature:
Date:	Date:

Kathmandu Upatyaka Khanepani Limited

Project Implementation Directorate

SITE INSPECTION FORM #214 A

Joint Monitoring with Contractor before Field Mobilization

Wastewater Treatment Plant

(confined area)

Purpose:	Review contractor's EMP/SEMP compliance preparations before field mobilization
Frequency:	Once before field mobilization and follow-up monitoring using monitoring checklist #214 B
Stage:	Contract awarded. Before mobilization, the contractor submits SEMP and OHS Plan for approval
Responsible:	Project staff/engineer and contractor's staff (PM, safeguard, and safety staff)- jointly
Date:	Time:

Project Detail

Contract package:	Weather (√):
Name of contractor:	
Name of site in-charge:	Municipality:
Name of safeguard/safety staff and others with contact no:	Ward No: Tole:
1.	3.
2.	4.

Technical Detail

Site area:	Soil Type (√): A B C
Proposed structures:	

Site topography (√): (i) Flat (ii) Rolling						
Land use (√):	Urban	Peri-urban	Rural	Heritage	Agri	Forest	Riverside

Drainage condition and probability of flooding:

Date to start construction:	Date to complete construction:	
SEMP/OHS Approved (√): Y N	Submission date:	Approval date:

Issues:			
SN	Issues	Y/N/NA	Remarks
Upfront activities are in place:			
1	Have all approvals/ permits from the government been is obtained? Any pending approvals with expected date?		
2	Are there any land acquisition-related issues? If yes, what is the status (compensation, deed transfer)?		
3	Is the site accessible? Any traffic-related issue? If yes, coordination with traffic police?		
4	Are there underground facility, overhead transmission line, or heritage area-related issues? What is the plan?		
5	Is the community informed of the work? Are there any community concerns? Any response by the project?		
6	Are their any sensitive receivers around the site? List.		
7	Has the contractor mobilized safeguard officer and safety officer? Was their curriculum vitae approved by the engineer?		
SEMP and OHS implementation arrangements (maps, resources, tools, and facilities):			
1	Site base map of camp facilities and sensitive receptors prepared.		
2	Site delineated, cleaned, fenced, and arrangements for guarding and lighting prepared.		
3	Plan to establish camp with cabins, kitchen, dinning, toilet (male and female), water supply, waste management, recreational facility, etc. at required standard prepared.		
4	Plan for camp and site management is prepared with groups formed and responsible person identified.		
5	Arrangements for health and safety of workers along with medical room, health worker, first aid, fire extinguisher, and emergency protocol considered in the OHS plan.		
6	Safety and informative signboards designed (in local language) as per the PID standards.		
7	On-site manual and vehicular movement path designated on the map.		
8	Plantation plan with nursery prepared for tree, garden, and greening of the area.		
9	Construction material stockpile and chemicals storage area identified and demarcated.		
10	Topsoil collection, and excavated material stockpile area arranged.		
11	Waste management system established.		
12	Arrangement for air, water, noise level test and location finalized in reference to sensitive receptors.		

SN	Issues	Y/N/NA	Remarks
13	Proper landscaping and drainage plan prepared.		
14	Tree plantation and vegetation plan prepared.		
15	Code of conduct for workers prepared and approved.		
16	Plan to manage the sludge is prepared and management location identified.		
17	EMP and OHS compliance monitoring checklist prepared.		
18	Contractor's routine reporting format and frequency agreed in the SEMP.		
Other issues if any?			
Any Particular Remark:			

Signature	Signature	Signature
Name and Position	Name and Position	Name and Position

Detailed Site Plan (sketch) with Structure Location and Sensitive Receptors

---

Note: Refer to Section- for the guidelines and instructions required for a site plan map

Kathmandu Upatyaka Khanepani Limited

Project Implementation Directorate

MONITORING SCORE SHEET #214 B

Joint Monitoring with Contractor during Construction

Wastewater Treatment Plant

(confined area)

Purpose:	Review contractor's EMP/SEMP compliance performance during work implementation
Frequency:	Daily/once a week (as required) when work is ongoing
Stage:	Construction stage and when work is ongoing at the particular site
Responsible:	Project staff/environment expert of engineer and contractor's staff (PM, safeguard, and safety staff)- jointly

Date:	Time:

Project Detail

Contract package:	Weather (√):
Name of contractor:	
Name of site in-charge:	Municipality:
Name of safeguard/safety staff and others with contact no:	Ward No: Tole:
1.	3.
2.	4.

Workers

Number of workers (number):	Female:	Male:	Child:

SN	Item	Activities	Yes (√)	No (√)	Full Score	Score Card	Corrective Action Agreed with Deadline
1	Occupational Health and Safety	Work implemented only when the site engineer/ supervisor and safety officer are present at site			2		
		Camp structure constructed, and facilities are provided as per the PID standard attached to the Contrat Agreement. No tarpaulin tents or old CGI sheet are used.			6		
		Few readymade tents at stock to use for isolation in case of emergency such as the COVID-19 infection.			1		
		Health of workers screened during intake, and periodic health check-up (twice a year) arranged.					

SN	Item	Activities	Yes (√)	No (√)	Full Score	Score Card	Corrective Action Agreed with Deadline
		% of workers using full set of PPEs (hard hat, reflective jacket, gloves, goggles, boot, face mask, safety belt, etc.).			3		
		Site fenced, guarded, people registered at entry in camp.			2		
		Work site is barricaded for preventing unauthorized entry, and signs like red flag, signboard placed to alert people.					
		Site landscaped with proper drainage system. No water pools in the site.			2		
		Separate movement path for people and vehicles clearly demarked inside the site.			2		
		First aid box at site at all time. Group leader trained in using first aid.			2		
		Medical room with full-time health worker arranged. Required emergency supplies and sick bed available. Standby vehicle in case of emergency.			4		
		Emergency contact person's name and number pasted in the camp and available to workers.			1		
		Emergency assembly point demarcated.			1		
		Health of workers screened during intake, and periodic health check-up (twice a year).			2		
		Fire extinguisher available at site and camp and workers trained to use them.			2		
		Double insulated wire used at work areas and camp			3		
		Use of double-insulated wire in both work site and labor camp.			5		
		Are guard rail and three board working platform arranged during work at height?			5		
		Storage of diesel, chemicals with impervious floor with drain discharging in collector pit and spill kit are kept ready.					
		Shoring done in deep excavations 1-meter depth.			5		
		Construction material kept at minimum 2 meters distance away from trench.			2		

SN	Item	Activities	Yes (√)	No (√)	Full Score	Score Card	Corrective Action Agreed with Deadline
		Construction materials (cement, aggregate, rebar, scaffolding, formwork, fuel and lubricant) and waste stockpiled properly at designated location.			3		
		Operational procedure for use of construction equipment is prepared and provided to worker.			2		
		Site area/path is clean of nail, rods, bricks, and other sharp materials for safety of workers.			3		
		Chemical and fuel stored properly (impervious platform with drain/sump well, spill kit available).			2		
		Cement slurry, chemicals, oils are not discharged over the ground but collected in collection pit and properly disposed without harming the environment or human health.			2		
2	Noise, Air and Water Quality	Noise level monitored at agreed frequency near sensitive receptor neighboring the area.			2		
		Earplug used by workers at noisy area.			2		
		Drinking water supplied at camp and work site tested at agreed frequency.			2		
		Water reserved for 48 hours at all time.			2		
		Volumetric air sampler placed near sensitive receptor and measured at required intervals.			2		
		Water spraying done to suppress dust (3-4 times a day) as instructed by the engineer.			4		
3	Signage	Standard signboard for safety, SOP, traffic prepared as per the PID standards and placed at the right location.			2		
		Safety board clearly showing use of PPEs, any risks and hazardous areas.					
4	Community Safety	Grievance register kept at site and office.			3		
		Common access road kept clean of potholes and dust if used by project vehicle.			2		
		Consultation with community conducted at regular interval through various media.			2		

SN	Item	Activities	Yes (√)	No (√)	Full Score	Score Card	Corrective Action Agreed with Deadline
5	Solid Waste	Solid waste at camp and work area properly segregated, collected, and disposed. Burning is restricted.			3		
6	Sanitation Facilities	Sufficient number of toilet and bath with water arranged for male and female.			2		
		Toilet wastes discharged into properly constructed two-chamber septic tank.			2		
		Bathing/washing/cooking water discharged into sewer or soak-pit.			2		
		Separate kitchen and dining provided. No cooking and eating inside cabins.			2		
		Site is well landscaped and drained. No water pools in the area.			2		
		TOTAL			**100**		
		TOTAL (%)					

Notes:

1. If the work is being done in confined space, then confined space checklist needs to be filled.

2. Assign points of high importance to certain "Activities" and if even half score is not met for those points, the total scoring could be considered as not met the requirement even if all the other points are met.

On behalf of PID and Consultant	On behalf of the contractor
Name and Position:	**Name and Position:**
Signature:	**Signature:**
Date:	**Date:**

Kathmandu Upatyaka Khanepani Limited

Project Implementation Directorate

Kathmandu Upatyaka Khanepani Limited

Project Implementation Directorate

ENVIRONMENTAL AUDIT FORM #215

Wastewater Treatment Plant
(Confined Area)

Purpose:	Conduct environmental audit of the quality of safeguard and OHS performance
Frequency:	Once a year or as and when required
Stage:	Construction stage and operation stage
Responsible:	Environmental expert of the employer

Performed by	
Date	
Location	

Compliance category:

Category	Explanation	Action Required
Complied (C)	Meets requirements	Document evidence that demonstrates compliance. No further action.
Opportunity for improvement (OFI)	Requirement met; however, it is not best practice. This may result in environmental harm or breaches of legislation if improvements are not made in the future.	Undertake risk assessment to identify potential for noncompliance. Identify and document opportunities for improvement if required.
Minor noncompliance (NC-Min)	Requirement has not been met; however, no environmental harm is evident or the potential for environmental harm as a result is low.	Action is required to make sure that requirement is met within a specified time period, which is written on the checklist.
Major noncompliance (NC-Maj)	Requirement has not been met and there is a significant risk of environmental harm or environmental harm has occurred as a result.	Immediate action is required to rectify the situation. Re-analyse within 4 weeks to ensure the corrective action has been successful. The EPA must also be notified as soon as reasonably practicable if the harm is considered serious or material.

Sample Environmental Audit Form

Activities	Impacts Predicted	Mitigation Measures suggested by EMP/ SEMP	Audit Checklist	C	OFI	NC-Min	NC- Maj	Action Recommended
I. Pre-Construction Phase								
Institutional	Weak safeguard mechanism	▪ Safeguard mechanism	▪ Confirm if safeguard mechanism is established and functional. ▪ Confirm full team of required experts are planned to be mobilized from the project, consultant, and contractors.					
Permit and approval	Disruptions of existing WWTP during work	▪ Obtain required permits and approval for disruption of existing wastewater treatment plant.	▪ All permits obtained in time. ▪ Project was delayed by_____ days/not delayed due to timely obtaining of permits					
Public consultations	Social stress	▪ Develop and implement a project communication plan.	▪ Annual communications plan was prepared before initiation of work. ▪ Stakeholders were consulted as per the plan. ▪ Final designs, safeguard measures and other project information were disseminated.					
Camp, quarry, and disposal sites are identified and approved	Poor camp standard Poor site with risk of landslide, flood, etc.	▪ Take approval of local authority to establish camp (both main and site camp). ▪ Camp standards as per contract with safety, healthy living, eating, medical, and recreational facilities ▪ Disposal sites are stable, and properly planned. ▪ Quarry site is identified, quarry operation plan is prepared, and clearance is taken.	▪ Camp, quarry, spoil disposal sites are as per approved location and design. ▪ Camp has facilities as per the standard, with all required sanitary and living facilities provided . ▪ Camp area is placed at a secure and stable site.					

Activities	Impacts Predicted	Mitigation Measures suggested by EMP/SEMP	Audit Checklist	C	OFI	NC–Min	NC– Maj	Action Recommended
II. Construction Phase								
Physical Environment								
Earthwork/ topsoil stripping and excavation for trenches	Loss of organic topsoil Soil erosion and slope destabilization	■ Stockpile topsoil for reuse ■ Spoil disposal at designated sites ■ Zero soil approach ■ Backfill trench, temporary sealing ■ Avoid work during the rainy days ■ Provide proper drainage ■ Prevent sediment flow to river	■ Top soil reuse ■ Spoil sites approved by the engineer and managed (no. of sites and volume managed) ■ Zero soil approach strictly followed with work area clean of dust ■ No pothole and waterlogging on trenches ■ Trenches back fill requiring sometime to lay permanent surface have temporary sealing ■ Pedestrian and traffic do not have hardship and are informed of work. ■ Clean worksite with good housekeeping to avoid sediment flow in water bodies					

Activities	Impacts Predicted	Mitigation Measures suggested by EMP/SEMP	Audit Checklist	C	OFI	NC-Min	NC- Maj	Action Recommended
Site and camp establishment	Camp needs to be as per agreed standards.	■ Poor quality structure ■ Poor living condition ■ Impact on physical and mental health of workers	■ Are the labor camp constructed of prefabricated structure or old CGI sheet on bamboo frame ■ Are fences, gates, lighting, safe zone, information board, safety signs in required number and in good condition? ■ Are all types of hazards at the site identified and area cleared and protection measures considered? ■ Camp has medical facility. ■ Kitchen, dinning, laundry, toilet and bathing facility are available					
Handling of waste and materials	Water pollution	■ Cement slurry, chemicals do not reach water bodies or on open ground ■ Toilets with septic tanks ■ Storage of construction aggregates, hazardous materials in safe areas ■ Prohibit washing of vehicles in rivers ■ Recover used oil and lubricants and reuse or remove from the sites ■ Keep fuel, lubricant away from river ■ Workshop/generator on impervious floor	■ Water quality test of water bodies near concrete mixture, worksites. ■ Sediment and oil trap provided around material storage area and workshops ■ No. of toilet for each worker at camp ■ Mobile toilet provided at worksite ■ Material stockpile yard at designated location ■ Prohibition/restrictive signage is sufficient, clean, and readable. ■ Generator and chemicals are kept covered and over impervious floor with drainage to trap any accidental spill.					

Activities	Impacts Predicted	Mitigation Measures suggested by EMP/ SEMP	Audit Checklist	C	OFI	NC-Min	NC- Maj	Action Recommended
Operation of machineries, vehicles, and equipment	Air pollution Dust pollution Noise nuisance Safety	■ Dust suppression by sprinkling water ■ Cover materials during transportation ■ Limit vehicle speed to 10–15 kilometers per hour. ■ Monitor vehicle emission. ■ Regular maintenance of vehicles ■ Ventilate confined working area ■ Monitor air, water, and noise levels. ■ Human and vehicle movement path ■ No horn in settlement areas.	■ Air quality (SOX, NOX, CO_2, CO) routinely measured and within standard limit. ■ Dust (PM_{10}, $PM_{2.5}$) routinely measured and within standard limit. ■ Stockpiles covered during transportation or storage. ■ Speed limit followed by drivers. ■ Road safety issue or accident. ■ Vehicles used are well maintained and emission tested regularly. ■ Ventilators in confined spaces.					
Operation of machineries, vehicles, and equipment Horn honking	Noise pollution Vibration	■ Monitor noise levels regularly at site. ■ Use silencer in heavy machineries. ■ Limit vehicle speed. ■ Restrict power horns. ■ Maintain equipment and vehicle. ■ Monitor damage to old houses. and structures by vibration.	■ Noise level (dba) monitored near sensitive receptors. ■ Vehicles use silencer. ■ Vehicle limit is followed within camp and on public road. ■ Power horns are restricted. ■ Asset inventory at sensitive locations prepared and monitored for any damage from vibration.					

Activities	Impacts Predicted	Mitigation Measures suggested by EMP/ SEMP	Audit Checklist	C	OFI	NC-Min	NC- Maj	Action Recommended
Drainage management	Flooding at camp and work sites Vector disease	▪ Site is surveyed for levels and landscaping plan prepared ▪ Drainage plan is prepared and drainage system functional ▪ Surface water collected in sump pit before discharging in water body	▪ Camp and work sites are free of water pool. ▪ Surface water is drained in a settling tank to filter sediment before discharging in natural water body. ▪ No community protest due to unmanaged drainage outfall.					
Biological Environment								
Vegetation clearance	Loss of green coverage	▪ Compensatory and greenery promotion plantation. ▪ Do not use firewood for cooking and heating.	▪ Is plantation plan prepared? ▪ Has nursery been arranged? ▪ Has plantation been carried out? ▪ What is the rate of survival of planted saplings? ▪ Riverbank plantation is also planned?					
Socioeconomic and Cultural Environment								
Work environment	Occupational health and safety	▪ Workers camp as per the PID standard (fence, kitchen, dining, toilet, water, electricity) ▪ Medical facility with a health worker ▪ Regular health checkup and workers insurance ▪ Training workers (safety, health, HIV) ▪ Safety signboards ▪ Use of PPE, and compensate for injuries	▪ Camp standard and facility approved by the engineer. ▪ Medical facility established. ▪ Health worker supporting the medical facility. ▪ Workers have been insured. ▪ Workers are given orientation on safety to be followed while carrying out work. ▪ Safety signboards placed at site. ▪ % of PPEs use. ▪ Any injury or fatality, and compensation measure.					

Activities	Impacts Predicted	Mitigation Measures suggested by EMP/ SEMP	Audit Checklist	C	OFI	NC-Min	NC- Maj	Action Recommended
Construction activity	Damage of infrastructure and community services	▪ Reinstate damaged community assets (electric pole, telephone lines, WS, sewerage lines, roads). ▪ Arrange temporary service until disruption. ▪ Regular community consultation.	▪ Reinstatement record of infrastructures ▪ Arrangement of temporary service ▪ Record of community complaint					
Construction activity	Traffic disruption	▪ Manage traffic seeking help of traffic police ▪ Install safety and traffic signals, if required around the WWTP site. ▪ Operationalize GRM.	▪ Consultation record with traffic police office ▪ If local people were informed ▪ If signboards and informatory boards placed at site					
Construction activity	Employment to local people	▪ Employ local people especially affected families and women ▪ No gender-biased wage rate ▪ No child labor	▪ Number of locals employed ▪ Wage rate to male and female ▪ Any case of child labor					
Outside workers in the project	Increase in social stress, crime, and conflict	▪ Prohibit gambling and alcohol in the camp. ▪ Instruct the workforce to respect the local cultures, traditions, rights. ▪ Provide security in contractors camp. ▪ Provide recreational facility in camp.	▪ Record of social disharmony and crime ▪ Record of awareness to workers ▪ Restrictions to workers ▪ Workers/staff follows code of conduct ▪ Community responses					
III. Operation Phase								

Activities	Impacts Predicted	Mitigation Measures suggested by EMP/ SEMP	Audit Checklist	C	OFI	NC-Min	NC-Maj	Action Recommended
Discharge of industrial wastes to WWTS	D/S pollution, health, and environmental risks	■ Train workers on OHS hazards. ■ Provide PPE. ■ Monitor illegal discharge of industrial wastes to the system. ■ Enforce regulation	■ Number of training on waste hazard and participants list ■ Use of PPE ■ Monitoring at the inlet of WWTP for electrical conductivity and DO ■ Action taken on illegally discharging industries					
Wastewater treated	Sludge generation	■ Safe disposal of sludge	■ Review how sludge is being managed. ■ Resource recovery is practiced. ■ Residual sludge reused such as to reclaim land.					
Release of wastewater to river	D/S pollution, health, and environmental risks	■ Treat wastewater to meet the effluent standards before releasing in river. ■ Test quality of the treated wastewater and river water.	■ Review record of quality of treated wastewater that will be released to river TSS, BOD, and heavy metals in mg/l, pH, T(^{0}C).					
Overflow flooding	Public and environmental health hazards	■ Careful O&M of wastewater system. ■ Provide stand-by generators for uninterrupted power. ■ Train operators.	■ Ensure standby generators of sufficient capacity at site. ■ Emergency response system is operational. ■ O&M schedules is prepared and being followed. ■ Number of training type and participants.					
Sewer cleaning	Risk of communicable diseases	■ Provide trainings to workers on OHS	■ Number of trainings conducted ■ Arrangements made to safely contain and treat communicable diseases, if they occur.					

Name:

Signature:

Date:

Mobile No:

Kathmandu Upatyaka Khanepani Limited
Project Implementation Directorate

Labor Camp Monitoring Checklist #216

Project:	Location:	Date:

Evaluation Items	Performance Criteria	Score Allocated*	Monitoring Detail (Insert information recorded during monitoring)	Urgent Corrective Actions	Score achieved
Campsite (15)	Local level clearance taken to locate camp.	1			
	Camp located at least 300 feet away from water course and waterbodies.	1			
	Camp not inside forest, sensitive ecosystems or heritage area.	1			
	Camp area is kept clean and sanitary from debris and garbage.	2			
	Camp is safe from potential flooding and erosion/slide.	2			
	Camp area is well drained and free from stagnant water pool, potholes where vector can breed.	2			
	Camp has a management committee and camp-in-charge is appointed.	2			
	Camp location does not have social dispute or complaint.	2			
	Camp accessible by road. Access road is graveled or sealed, kept maintained, and water sprayed 4 times a day.	2			
				Subtotal:	

Evaluation Items	Performance Criteria	Score Allocated*	Monitoring Detail (Insert information recorded during monitoring)	Urgent Corrective Actions	Score achieved
Camp Structure and Cabins/ Rooms **(25)**	Camp structure is as per PID standard and approved by the engineer. Old corrugated galvanized iron (CGI) sheet and tarpaulin with wooden frame for main or makeshift site camp is prohibited.	5			
	The floor is elevated above flood level, impervious, and drained.	2			
	The roof is watertight, colored GI or PVC sheet used. No CGI/tarpaulin.	2			
	What is the ratio of number of people in the camp vis a vis number or rooms available (not more than 4:1 in a 12 feet x 10 feet room)?	2			
	What is room size and how many persons are sleeping in a room (should not be more than 8 persons)?	2			
	What are the sizes of door and windows in a room (door should not be less than 6 feet x 3 feet; 20 square feet window opening for a room of 12 feet x 10 feet and natural light)?	3			
	Do the rooms have light, fan, bed and bedding, and mosquito net for each bed?	3			
	What is the type of bed provided (double decker not used)?	2			
	Recreation facility provided (outdoor sport, TV room)?	2			
				Subtotal:	
Kitchen and Dining **(10)**	Are kitchen, dining, and store in separate shed from residential cabins?	2			
	Is the floor elevated above flood level?	2			
	Are cooking and eating on floor and in the cabins/ rooms prohibited?	1			
	Number of dinning tables and chairs provided (>1 chair for 2 persons)?	1			
	How is food cooked (firewood, LPG?)?	1			
	Is safe drinking water provided?	1			
	How and where is wastewater drained?	2			
				Subtotal:	

Evaluation Items	Performance Criteria	Score Allocated*	Monitoring Detail (Insert information recorded during monitoring)	Urgent Corrective Actions	Score achieved
Drinking Water Supply and Storage (10)	Is drinking water safe and clean (tested)?	4			
	Is drinking water available is (>10 liters per day per person)?	3			
	Is water for other uses supplied is (>80 liters water/day/person)?	3			
Solid Waste Management (5)	Waste collected and segregated. Landfill constructed at site or waste given to municipal waste collector. Waste is not burned.	3			
	How many waste containers are provided in camp and kitchen? Sufficient?	1			
	When was last de-pesting, spraying for vector control carried out?	1			
				Subtotal:	
Toilet Facility (8)	How many toilets for men and how many for women provided in the camp (is it <1:15)?	2			
	Which material is used for construction of toilets? What is the size?	1			
	Are toilets connected to sewer, septic tank or directly discharged into river?	2			
	What is the distance of toilets from cabins (>100 feet)?	1			
	Is water and handwash basin available near toilets?	1			
	What is the schedule of cleaning of toilets? Who cleans them?	1			
				Subtotal:	
Electricity and Lighting (2)	Double insulated wires are used. Circuit breakers or fuse protections in use to protect against any electrical hazard.	1			
	Orientation to treat electric shock is given to staff and workers.	1			
				Subtotal:	

Evaluation Items	Performance Criteria	Score Allocated*	Monitoring Detail (Insert information recorded during monitoring)	Urgent Corrective Actions	Score achieved
Medical Facility in Labor Camp (20)	First aid kit available at camp and work sites	2			
	A medical facility with sick bed is arranged inside the camp.	4			
	Is there any medical personnel supporting the medical facility?	2			
	How is workers' health screened during intake and while in work?	2			
	Is there an emergency protocol established with name and number of safety staff and camp in-charge, site engineer to contact in case of injury and accidents?	3			
	Is the COVID-19 prevention plan or SOP being followed?	2			
	When was last health camp organized in the camp	1			
	Is first aid application training given to workers	1			
	Has contractor given orientation to their staff and worker on STD, HIV/AIDS	1			
	Are the workers insured	2			
				Subtotal:	
Fire Fighting Facility in Camp (5)	How many fire extinguishers, fire grenades or fire buckets are kept at camp? Is it sufficient?	2			
	Date expired fire extinguishers are timely replaced? When was the workers given training to use the fire fighting equipment?	2			
	Is there a standby pump and long hose kept ready for emergency?	1			
				Subtotal:	
		100		**Total Score**	

Note: Give score based on quality of compliance. Scoring can be used at multiples of 0.5.

Kathmandu Upatyaka Khanepani Limited

Project Implementation Directorate

ACCIDENT / INJURY REPORT
FORM #217

ADB Loan: **Loan : Kathmandu Valley ....Project**

Client: Project Implementation Directorate (PID)

Kathmandu Upatyaka Khanepani Limited (KUKL)

Anamnagar, Kathmandu, Nepal

Contractor: ....

Contract Package: ....

Consultant: ....

A. Accident Details

Accident Date and Time: ....at approx ....am/pm

Victims Name: ....

1. Introduction:

Present brief background and detail of the accident.

2. Name of Persons Present in the Team

S.No	Name of Staff	Designation	Remarks

3. Chronology of Events

Time	Detail of Incident
Approx .... Am/ Pm	
Approx .... Am/ Pm	
Approx .... Am/ Pm	

4. Action Taken Immediately After the Accident

Time	Chronological Detail of Incident
Approx .... Am/Pm	
Approx .... Am/Pm	
Approx .... Am/Pm	

5. Measures Taken

1. Incident Investigation: ....
2. Compensation: ....

B. Follow-Up Safety Measures Placed in the Project

1. Safeguards Compliance

Government of Nepal (GoN) and ADB have vetted the Environmental Management Plan (EMP) to be included in the bidding documents and the contracts of civil works packages under the project. The EMP outlines occupational health and safety measures to be taken during implementation, which are in line with international best practices. The implementing agency, PID/KUKL conducts both internal and external monitoring and reports are disclosed on the website (refer: ADB's website for the project safeguards monitoring reports: https://www.adb.org/projects/34304-043/main#project-documents). ADB undertakes comprehensive project review missions, including site inspections and periodically monitors project sites. PID/ADB also supports training contractors, consultants and implementing agency staff on EMP compliance. When incidents of non compliance are identified, PID Safeguards Unit along with ADB meets with contractors and implementing agency staff to agree on corrective measures.

2. Safeguards and Safety Compliance by Contractor

List training provided to staff and worker...............

List safety mechanism including assurance by contractor and reporting.....................................

Arrangements made in project in case of accidents. Confirm if the procedure was following this case..........................

3. Safeguards and Safety Compliance Monitored and Ensured by Consultant

The Consultant has established a safeguard compliance and Health & Safety mechanism in the project. They have mobilized a senior Environment Consultant to monitor safeguard compliance and safety compliance. The .... Engineer reviews safety preparation compliance by the contractor before executing specific work. No work related with operation of heavy equipment, deep trenching, work at height, work in confined space etc. are allowed without screening by and presence of safety officer, and medical facility at standby. Regular monitoring of all site is done by the consultant, with verbal and written instruction to contractors to maintain safety. The monitoring is carried out using standard checklist and monthly reported to employer. The Regular Meetings and workshops are organized and "notice to correct" type of letters are also issued by the Engineer to enforce the culture of safeguards and safety amongst contractors.

C.   Others

1. Labor Law Compliance:

ADB's policies as the Social Protection Strategy (2001) require that the government labor laws or internationally recognised core labor laws are complied within the projects supported by ADB. The loan agreement for the KVWSIP specifies that the project must comply with Borrower's Labor laws. The minimum legal working age in Nepal is 16 years (Nepal Child Labor Act, 2003). [https://www.adb.org/sites/default/files/project-document/60546/34304-04-nep-dfj.pdf]

2. Photographic Details

Kathmandu Upatyaka Khanepani Limited

Project Implementation Directorate

GRIENVANCE REDRESS MECHANISM

Schematic Diagram #218

Schematic Diagram of Grievance Redress Mechanism

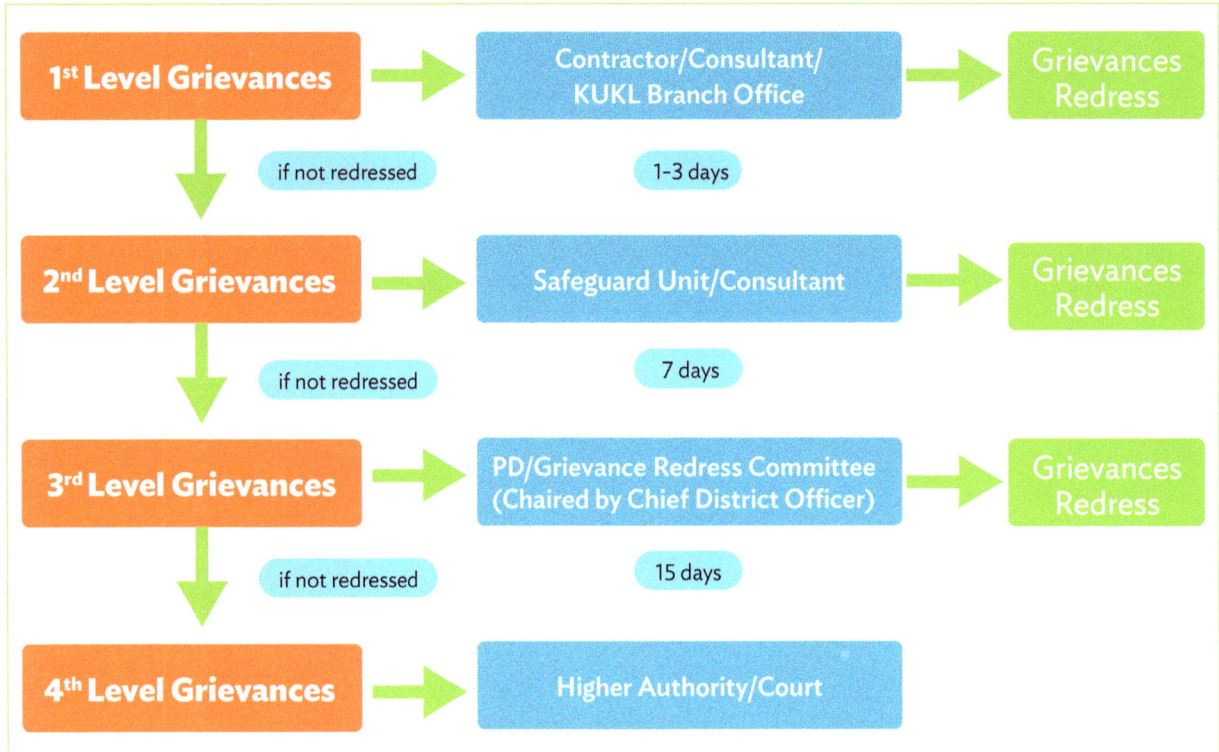

1st Level Grievances	→	Contractor/Consultant/ KUKL Branch Office	→	Grievances Redress
↓ if not redressed		1-3 days		
2nd Level Grievances	→	Safeguard Unit/Consultant	→	Grievances Redress
↓ if not redressed		7 days		
3rd Level Grievances	→	PD/Grievance Redress Committee (Chaired by Chief District Officer)	→	Grievances Redress
↓ if not redressed		15 days		
4th Level Grievances	→	Higher Authority/Court		

Kathmandu Upatyaka Khanepani Limited

Project Implementation Directorate

Heritage Impact Assessment/Chance Find Procedure Form #219

Excavation of trenches for construction could uncover movable artifacts, for example smaller relics, idols, and building fragments, or immovable archaeology such as building foundations, walls, or wells. Care must be taken in the excavation in order to identify chance finds before any damage occurs. These methods are outlined in the construction specifications.

The following procedures outline the protocol for all project actors to follow in the case that movable or immovable objects are discovered during construction of the project. These procedures provide a guideline, but ultimately any steps taken will depend on the situation and will be up to the discretion of the archaeologist of the Design and Supervision Consultant (DSC) with concurrence of concerned government agency (Department of Archaeology [DOA]).

The procedures are structured as the following:

Attachment A. Chance Finds Procedure for Movable Artifacts

Attachment B: Chance Finds Procedure for Immovable Archaeological Remains

Attachment C: Standard Archiving and Removal Guidelines

Attachment D: Heritage Impact Assessment Framework

Attachment A: Chance Finds Procedure for Movable Artifacts

Step 1	Discovery and Reporting Find of Movable Object(s)
1.1	Potential artifact uncovered during excavation.
1.2	Laborer notifies site supervisor in charge.
1.3	Site supervisor stops work in that segment immediately.
1.4	Site supervisor notifies archaeologist of the DSC /DOA immediately after stopping work.
Step 2	**Expert Inspection and Recommend Action**
2.1	DOA/archaeologist of supervision consultant inspects site immediately after notification.
2.2	Based on inspection, DOA determines if Archaeologist Expert Committee (AEC) meeting is necessary based on significance/complexity of find (e.g., ceramic fragment vs. large sculpture).
	If AEC required to meet, proceed to Step 3.
	If AEC not required to meet, proceed to Step 4.
Step 3	**Convene Archaeology Expert Committee**
3.1	AEC convenes at the site of archaeological finds within 24 hours at a time set by the DOA.
3.2	AEC investigates the site and holds briefing meeting after site visit at the DOA's premises.
3.3	AEC recommends either following Standard Archiving and Removal Guidelines, or agrees on any additional requirements depending on the type of find.
3.4	DSC archaeologist drafts meeting minutes signed by all members present.
Step 4	**Archiving and Removal of Artifacts**
4.1	Contractor archaeologist drafts any necessary method statements for excavation, handling, and/or removal of objects.
4.2	DSC approves method statements once the archaeologist and engineer are satisfied.
4.3	DSC with concurrence of the DOA authorizes the contractor to proceed with removal of artifacts following Standard Archiving and Removal Guidelines (see Attachment C), with any additional requirements determined by the AEC (if meeting took place).
4.4	Archiving and removal are supervised by the DSC archaeologist and DOA representative, providing field assistance as necessary.
4.5	DSC authorizes work to resume with concurrence of the DOA representative.
Step 5	**Reporting**
5.1	Reporting procedures to be followed in the Standard Archiving and Removal Guidelines (Attachment C).

Attachment B: Chance Finds Procedure for Immovable Archaeological Remains

Step 1	Discovery and Reporting Find of Archaeological Remains
1.1	Potential artifact uncovered during excavation.
1.2	Laborer notifies site supervisor in charge.
1.3	Site supervisor stops work in that segment immediately.
1.4	Site supervisor notifies archaeologist of the DSC /DOA immediately after stopping work.
Step 2	**Expert Inspection and Recommend Action**
2.1	DOA/DSC inspect site immediately after notification.
2.2	Based on inspection, DOA/archaeologist of the DSC determine if find is archaeology and, if so, convenes AEC meeting.
	If AEC required to meet, proceed to Step 3.
	If AEC not required to meet, DSC authorizes work to resume with concurrence of DOA.
Step 3	**Convene Archaeology Expert Committee**
3.1	AEC convenes at the site of archaeological finds within 24 hours at a time set by DOA.
3.2	AEC investigates the site and holds briefing meeting after site visit at DOA's premises.
3.3	AEC develops an Archaeological Action Plan within 48 hours. The plan should decide on the following options and will provide detailed procedures as needed depending on the find (in addition to the Standard Archiving and Removal Guidelines):
A	Leave archaeology intact and avoid area. ■ For cases where finds are significant and highly unique, and construction would cause irreparable harm to archaeology. The subsurface investigation conducted prior to works should identify any significant archaeology prior to excavation, however significant finds could still be possible. ■ Alternative route must be found. ■ Site is archived then covered and reinstated unless a plan for immediate further study is agreed.
B	Remove remains temporarily and restore following pipeline installation ■ Most likely for any finds above the installed pipe. ■ Agreement must be reached on temporary storage site (either Museum or DOA premises, depending on type of find). ■ Agree on any further study to be done while remains are removed. ■ Determine if method statement need to be prepared for excavation, handling, and/or reinstating remains .

C	Remove remains permanently and archive.
	■ Most likely for any finds that would be bisected by the installed pipe.
	■ Agreement must be reached on temporary storage site during removal and archiving (either Patan Museum or DOA premises, depending on type of find).
	■ Agree on any method statements needed for excavation, handling, etc.; DSC to issue instructions.
	■ Action plan should include next steps for reaching an agreement on permanent location/curation of removed assets, which may not be possible until the excavation has taken place.
D	Other option (or combination of the above) as determined by the AEC
3.4	Archaeologist of DSC drafts meeting minutes signed by all members present.
	If decision B, C, and D taken, proceed to Step 4.
Step 4	**Archiving and Removal of Artifacts**
4.1	Archaeologist of DSC holds site meeting with the contractor to brief them on Archaeology Action Plan. Archaeologist of the DSC prepares meeting minutes and instructions to the contractor.
4.2	Contractor archaeologist drafts any necessary method statements for excavation, handling, and/or removal of objects.
4.3	Archaeologist of DSC approves method statements once the archaeologist and engineer are satisfied.
	DSC authorizes the contractor to proceed with implementing the Archaeology Action Plan. Standard Archiving and Removal Guidelines must be followed (see Attachment C), with any additional requirements determined by the AEC's Action Plan.
4.4	Archiving and removal are supervised by the archaeologist of the DSC and the DOA representative, providing field assistance as necessary.
Step 5	**Reporting**
5.1	Reporting procedures to be followed in the Standard Archiving and Removal Guidelines (Attachment C).

Attachment C: Standard Archiving and Removal Guidelines

These guidelines should be followed by the DSC, Contractor and/or other field archaeologists designated to assist in the archiving and removal of archaeological remains and/or movable artifacts. Note that authorization to proceed with the removal of any artifacts must be granted by the DSC with concurrence of DOA per the Chance Finds Procedures. These procedures are a minimum guideline, and may be supplemented by additional procedures, methods, or specifications as agreed by the Archaeology Expert Committee (AEC), DOA, and/or Archaeologist of DSC.

1	**Documentation in Situ**
1.1	Upon exposure, archaeological remains or artifacts should be fully documented by the contractor at the site of discovery, including photographs with time/date stamps, measurements and drawings.
1.2	The contractor takes GPS points at the point of discovery.
1.3	The DOA and AEC may recommend that the contractor carry out additional environmental sampling (e.g., soil samples).
2	**Excavation**
2.1	Excavation may only proceed at the instruction of the DSC archaeologist (through the engineer), with the concurrence of DOA.
2.2	Excavation must be in the presence of a DOA representative and the DSC archaeologist.
2.3	Excavation in any area with chance finds must be done using manual digging.
2.4	Depending on the find, the contractor engineer will propose method statements for excavation, which must be approved by the DSC archaeologist.
2.5	The contractor and DSC should document excavation with photographs and video.
2.6	Excavation should follow any additional procedures as required by the AEC.
3	**Handling, Transport, and Storage**
3.1	Upon investigation of the DOA or the AEC (depending on the type of find) will determine if finds will be temporarily stored at the DOA Lalitpur branch office or the Patan Museum. This will be communicated to the contractor before removal.
3.2	Once removed, smaller objects may only be handled by a qualified archaeologist until official handover to DOA. Larger and/or more complex objects (e.g., foundations) may be handled by laborers under close supervision and instruction of the contractor/DSC/DOA archaeologist.
3.3	Objects must be stored in a secure, clean, lockable space.
3.4	Any unauthorized removal of archaeological materials will result in immediate dismissal from job duties and be subject to fines by DOA.

4	**Cleaning**
4.1	The excavated finds should be properly cleaned with water, except.
	i. if the finds are identified for scientific analysis by the DOA or AEC;
	ii. metal & organic objects (e.g., bone, wood, leather, textile objects, and etc.) should not be cleaned with water.
	The Contractor is advised to consult another member of the AEC, if in doubt.
5	**Marking**
5.1	The excavated finds should be cleaned before marking object number.
5.2	Each find should be marked with site code, context number and find number, etc.
5.3	For the finds that are too small, organic objects (e.g., bone, wood, leather, textile objects and etc.) or have unstable surface, object number should not be marked on the object directly. These finds should be bagged separately and attached with a label containing information about the site code, context number, find number, and description of find.
6	**Documentation Post-removal**
6.1	The contractor's archaeologist is responsible for documenting chance finds post-removal, unless otherwise agreed with the DSC.
6.2	After cleaning, smaller finds should be photographed on all sides on a plain white background, with date/time reference.
6.3	Measurements should be taken and recorded, and any drawings as needed.
7	**Labeling and Bagging (if necessary)**
7.1	Two labels should be provided for each bag, which contains find-sone is adhered on the surface of the bag, while the other is kept inside the bag for easy reference.
7.2	The label inside the bag should be kept separately with a smaller plastic bag so that the label can be kept much longer.
7.3	Information about the site code, context number, test-pit number, object number (or bag number), and description of finds should be written clearly on the label.
7.4	Finds under the same context should be bagged together. If those finds, however, have been categorized according to their typology, materials, or characteristics, separate bagging is required.

8	**Reporting and Handover Procedure**
8.1	All records should be handed over to the DOA, PID, municipality and DSC as a single organized archive within 7 days of completion of the removal. The contractor should ensure: ■ All the field records should be submitted together with indexes. ■ Any video footage should be submitted together with index describing the content of the video footage. ■ All photographs should be submitted together with photo register. ■ Any GPS/GIS maps should be handed over as coordinates and/or shapefiles. Field records include but are not limited to field diary, site record for trench excavation, context recording sheet, special finds recording sheet, soil sample and/or other environmental samples recording sheet, map (including GPS points, GIS shapefile), survey sheet, photograph/audio-visual records, etc. Finds processing records include conservation record, measured drawings, and photographs, laboratory reports, etc.
8.2	The contractor prepares two copies of a handover letter that lists all the aforementioned records, and handover details to DOA and copied to the PID, municipality, and DSC.
8.3	A representative of the DOA should be present when records and physical assets are handed over. The contractor representative should sign both copies of the letter, and the DOA representative should countersign. One copy will remain with the contractor, and one with DOA, and the contractor should provide scanned copies the PID, municipality, and DSC.
8.4	DSC archaeologist reviews the materials submitted by the contractor and drafts a chance finds report, which is annexed to the monthly progress report sent to the employer. This report is sent to the DOA Chief Archaeology Officer, the PID, and the municipality within 35 days of the find (per Ancient Monuments Preservation Act).
8.5	If considered appropriate by the Department of Archaeology, artefacts may be displayed in the museum.
8.6	A report on the findings of the excavation should be prepared and made available to researchers.

Attachment D: Heritage Impact Assessment Monuments but Not Declared Heritage Site

Cultural Heritage Inventory

.... Project

Contract Package: ....

Instructions:

- As part of the IEE, an inventory of cultural heritage areas and assets will be carried out for each of the DNIs to assess potential project impacts.

- This inventory should be completed for each Distribution Network Improvements (DNIs) to the best extent possible – it is not necessary to identify every small site, but we need to identify the types of heritage assets, locations, and potential impacts in each DNI.

- Where important sites or impacts are noted, be as specific as possible with the location, length of pipelaying that would impact an area, etc.

- Attach relevant photographs, maps, list of required government clearance and copy of legal provisions for ready reference

- Note any consultations with stakeholders held already where heritage issues were discussed in the table at the end of the form

SN	Category	Questions	Observations
1	**Heritage Areas**		
1.1	World Heritage Site (WHS) core zone	■ Will the ROW pass through WHS core zone? ■ If so, provide details on No of meters, the specific segments of pipelaying, and where in the WHS. ■ Include map of DNI overlaid with WHS core zone and buffer zone	
1.2	WHS buffer zone	■ Will the ROW pass through WHS buffer zone? ■ If so, provide details on No of meters, the specific segments of pipelaying, and provide physical details of site in the buffer zone.	
1.3	Tourism areas	■ Are there other touristic areas in the DNI ROW that are outside the WHS and buffer zone? If so describe. ■ Could these areas be disrupted by construction?	
1.4	Other heritage areas	■ Are there any other sensitive heritage areas (e.g., crematory, park/plaza, traditional religious/cultural and other community procession routes such as taking dead body to crematory etc.) that could be disrupted by construction?	

SN	Category	Questions	Observations
2	**Architecture and structures**		
2.1	Fragile structures at risk from construction activity	Are there any areas along the ROW with a concentration of fragile buildings? (e.g., old, damaged by earthquake)? If so, where are these areas and please provide some details on the approximate length of segments that would affect these areas.	
2.2	Major temples, Stupas, Bihars and cultural monuments	Provide names/locations of major religious/cultural structures along the ROW. Are there any sensitivities of construction activities around these temples?	
2.3	Roadside shrines and small temples	Are there roadside shrines along the ROW? Could any of these shrines be particularly sensitive (e.g., impede construction or be damaged)?	
2.4	Narrow roads	Are there any very narrow roads along the ROW (<3.5meters)? If so list and mark these areas in the attached map. Do these narrow roads coincide with heritage assets, fragile buildings, or roadside shrines?	
2.5	Flagstone/ traditional red bricks (TRB) (less or more than 100 years old) paving	Are there segments of the ROW with …… flagstone; …… TRB <100 years; >100 years flagstone paving? Note the approximate age and last time they were replaced If so, note location & approx. No of meters (needed for costing in BoQ)	
2.6	Other	List any other important structures to note	
3	**Traditional Water Infrastructure**		
3.1	Traditional water ponds or stone spouts	Are there traditional water ponds or stone spouts along the ROW? If so, provide names and locations Note any potential impacts of construction to these infrastructure.	
4	**Chance Finds**[3]		
4.1	Potential archaeological site	Are there any areas of potential archaeological interest and areas where archeological exploration/study was done in the past. Potential for small chance finds is anywhere – however areas with higher risk should be flagged for contractors to take extra precautions To find this information or support, consult with DOA, municipalities	

---

3   A chance find procedure is a project-specific procedure that outlines the actions to be taken if previously unknown cultural heritage is encountered (Guidance Note 8- Cultural Heritage 2012, IFC)

SN	Category	Questions	Observations
5	**Intangible heritage**		
5.1	Festivals/Rituals	Are there any festivals or Ritual times when project activities could adversely impact them? Please note the specific festivals/rituals, locations, and specific dates	

Attachment: Photographs and Maps

Description	Location	Map/Photograph

Consultations where heritage issues were discussed

Date	Stakeholders	Issues Discussed